# DEMOLISHING Demonic STRONGHOLDS

DESTINY IMAGE BOOKS BY DR. MORRIS CERULLO

*How to Pray*

*You Can Have a New Beginning*

*21 Days to Your Total Healing*

# DEMOLISHING Demonic STRONGHOLDS

SPIRITUAL FIREPOWER

Dr. Morris Cerullo

DESTINY IMAGE® PUBLISHERS, INC.
P.O. Box 310, Shippensburg, PA 17257-0310
*"Promoting Inspired Lives."*

Previously published as *One Demon Spirit*
by Morris Cerullo World Evangelism
Previous ASIN: B000HMQQHW

*You Can Know How to Defeat Satan*
by Morris Cerullo World Evangelism
Previous ASIN: B001PPTDCA

This book and all other Destiny Image, Revival Press, MercyPlace, Fresh Bread, Destiny Image Fiction, and Treasure House books are available at Christian bookstores and distributors worldwide.

For a U.S. bookstore nearest you, call 1-800-722-6774.
For more information on foreign distributors, call 717-532-3040.
Reach us on the Internet: www.destinyimage.com.

ISBN 13 TP: 978-0-7684-4193-2
ISBN 13 Ebook: 978-0-7684-8756-5

For Worldwide Distribution, Printed in the U.S.A.
4 5 6 7 8 / 16 15 14 13

# DEDICATION

This book is lovingly dedicated to Partners of World Evangelism who have become members of God's Victorious Army and share the vision God has given me to reach the world for Jesus Christ in these end times.

My prayer is that each of you will rise up with the greatest new anointing of God's power and spiritual breakthrough that you have ever known—that very same anointing that opens blind eyes, causes the deaf to hear and the lame to walk. Remember, "*...greater is He that is in you, than he that is in the world*" (1 John 4:4). If the enemy tries to come in like a flood, the spirit of the Lord God will raise up a standard against him (see Isaiah 59:19).

All my love and prayers.

God's servant,
Dr. Morris Cerullo

# CONTENTS

INTRODUCTION

# COULD A DEMON BE CONTROLLING YOUR LIFE?

DEMONIC POWER IS REAL. Do you believe it? I know you say that you do, but do you really believe that Satan's demons could be controlling your life right now?

I'm beginning to discover that even very dedicated Christians don't really understand what is happening to them in the spirit world. The other day I was deeply concerned when one of my most fervent ministry partners said to an associate of mine, "There's something about spiritual warfare that I just don't understand."

"What's that?" my associate replied.

"Well, Brother Cerullo says that, 'There is no total victory in spiritual war until we (as Christians) conquer our enemy who has already been defeated.' Now, I know that Satan is our enemy, and that demons do exist; but if Jesus already defeated them at Calvary two thousand years ago, why do we have to conquer them all over again? How could Satan have any real power over Christians if Jesus has already won?"

Unfortunately, this thinking is very common. On one hand, Christians are living lives of torment, walking in bondage and defeat with no real spiritual power. On the other hand, they know God's

Word and have been trained in spiritual warfare, but they have little idea of the power and the seriousness of the war they are in. The bottom line of all their thinking is, *Satan has already been stripped of his power. I'm safe because I'm in Jesus's hands.*

Beloved, if this is what you have been telling yourself, then you, too, have been blinded by one of the enemy's most brutal deceptions. Somehow, he has convinced you that all of the problems, illnesses, defeats, depressions, and anxieties in your life have nothing to do with demonic powers. He makes you think that they are all caused by circumstances, your in-laws, the wrong vitamins, a bad childhood, or anything else you can think of!

The fact is that demonic oppression is very real in the Church today.

There is one demon spirit that controls, dominates, possesses, oppresses, vexes, and torments eight out of ten people in the world today, including born-again Christians!

Right now there is an 80 percent chance that this demon spirit is secretly pulling you away from God, destroying your witness for Christ, and choking your growth in the Holy Spirit, and you don't even know it. Can you believe it?

I intend to prove it to you. Let us now turn to the Word of God, for God's infallible Word is the same yesterday, today, and forever.

CHAPTER 1

# WAS DEMONIC POWER REAL IN JESUS'S DAY?

THE BIBLE SAYS THAT ONE day a man came to Jesus and pleaded:

> *Sir, have mercy on my son, for he is mentally deranged, and in great trouble, for he often falls into the fire or into the water* (Matthew 17:15 TLB).

What was the boy's problem? Was it psychological? Hereditary? The Bible goes on to plainly state that he was vexed with a demon. For as soon as *"Jesus rebuked the demon in the boy...it left him, and from that moment the boy was well"* (Matthew 17:18 TLB).

Then, in the Gospel of Luke, we learn of a man from Gadara who was more than insane. When he came to meet Jesus, he was homeless, naked, and lived in a cemetery among the tombs. The demons took control of the man so often that even when he was shackled with chains, he simply broke them apart and rushed into the desert completely under the demons' power. When attacks and fits of demonic activity would come upon him, he would throw himself against rocks until his body was cut open and bleeding. When Jesus asked this demon his name, he replied, "Legion," because there were so many! (See Luke 8:27-31.)

Many people in this modern, sophisticated twenty-first century would say, "The poor man probably had a severe hormonal imbalance." Or, "I know that that kind of behavior is the result of a traumatic childhood." Or, "I guess he was just born a 'bad seed'."

That's not what the Bible says. The Bible says it was the work of demon spirits, pure and simple. The Word of God proves that this man was not just a bad seed or someone with a chemical problem, because when he was delivered of all of those foul spirits, he immediately became an outstanding evangelist (see Luke 8:33-39).

We could go on and on, proving in case after case that demonic power was real in Jesus's day. Not only was it real, but it severely tormented, oppressed, possessed, vexed, and controlled many people of biblical times. Demons caused deafness, blindness, and countless other ailments that destroyed the minds and bodies not only of the heathen, but of God's very own people.

## Is Demonic Power Real Today?

Now, I want you to take a little imaginary trip with me. Come into a mental institution for the insane, such as is found in many of your cities. I want you to take a good look around as we walk inside.

There's a woman who comes to greet us at the door. She's wearing a white uniform and has long keys dangling from her side. Let us have no delusions about what those keys unlock. They unlock cold, clammy, gray steel doors that house human beings just like you and I, people who are caged behind bars. You look inside one of those cages, and what do you see? You see a person just like you crouched against solid cement walls. On these walls you can see indentations—as deep as your fingers—that have been made by bleeding human hands.

Next, we walk to the place where they keep the "hard cases." There's one skinny little man there, and it is taking five men to get that one human being into a straitjacket.

Sound familiar? Like someone you just met in the country of Gadara in the Bible? Tell me, where do you think he gets his superhuman strength?

As we watch, we see that it takes one 250-pound male nurse to hold down each one of his arms, and two more to hold down his body and his legs. Meanwhile, another man tries to squeeze him into that straitjacket, the only thing that they have to control him. Why? Because that man is possessed with superhuman power.

That same superhuman, demonic power was as real 2,000 years ago as it is today. If you don't believe me, pick up your morning newspaper, and ask yourself—what makes a man, 19 years of age, strangle a beautiful young lady whom he has never seen before? What makes a young mother take her seven-day-old infant, stuff her into a trash can, close the lid, and leave her there to die?

The Bible tells us exactly what makes them do these things. It is the same demonic power that tried to murder that mentally deranged boy by throwing him into the fire! Again, we could go on and on with modern-day examples of demonic power and not even uncover the tip of the iceberg.

In Jesus's day, the reality of demonic power was never questioned. People knew it existed, pure and simple. The only thing that amazed them was that there was finally Someone around who had the power over the devil to do something about it. And do something He did. Jesus dealt with all of these gruesome situations in short order. How? With power and authority He commanded each one of those foul spirits to leave, and they did!

The public was astounded:

> ...*What new doctrine is this? For with authority He commands even the unclean spirits, and they obey Him* (Mark 1:27 NKJV).

By now you may be saying, "All right, Brother Cerullo, I've read my newspaper. I'll admit that Satan has great power in the world today. But all of those things I read about are with unsaved people. The devil can't get away with those atrocities in born-again

Christians. We're protected by the blood of the Lamb. Jesus died to save us from all of that."

You're absolutely right. Jesus did die to save us from all of that. However, all of that is still going on. Why?

Let me ask you a question. Do we have people in the Church today who are deaf? People who can't speak? People who have mental problems? People who are constantly ill?

Jesus has plainly shown us that many of these afflictions are a direct result of demonic oppression. (See Matthew 12:28,43; Mark 1:23,26; 7:25; 9:17-26; Luke 4:33; 8:29; 9:42 and 13:11.) In addition, we see the utter devastation caused by broken homes, child abuse, and divorce, which are rampant in the Church today. These are the very things that God sent His Son to this earth to destroy.

> *...For this purpose the Son of God was manifested, that He might destroy the works of the devil* (1 John 3:8 NKJV).

He then put all of the keys to spiritual power in our hands to finish the job. He has given us power over all of the power of the enemy (see Luke 10:19). Then why haven't we done something about all of those tormented, demon-oppressed brothers and sisters, sitting right next to us in the pews, as we listen to sermons about love week after week? My Bible says that just as Jesus is in heaven (the Everlasting Conqueror), so are we to be right now in this world (1 John 4:17).

Who is Jesus? He is the Victor. He is a Man of war against all of the destructive forces of the devil.

What are we? We are so bound and oppressed that I am concerned that many Christians are literally on their way to being spit out of His mouth! (See Revelation 3:16.)

## URGENT ALARM!

Today the Lord is urgently sounding the alarm, trying to make us see that many people in the Church who have assumed that they will be part of the Marriage Supper of the Lamb could instead be cast out of His Kingdom if they insist on living with the oppressive forces that are binding them and destroying Christ's Church. These oppressive forces are making you, as a Christian, both helpless and useless.

I want to read to you one of the most chilling stories in the Word of God. It is a story that haunts me day and night—a story that keeps me awake, grieving for God's blinded, oppressed, dominated, and controlled people.

I know of nothing that shows how a Christian can be rendered helpless, uselessly bound by Satan, more than the story Jesus Himself tells in Matthew 25:14-30. Open your Bible with me now as the Lord reveals to us the horrifying truth of how Satan oppresses God's people in the Church.

The story begins as Matthew tells of how the Master, Jesus, went away on a far journey. Before He left, He invested in His servants, entrusting them with all that He had.

Read this dramatic passage of Scripture with me now:

> *For the kingdom of heaven is as a man travelling into a far country, who called his own servants, and delivered unto them his goods.*
>
> *And unto one he gave five talents, to another two, and to another one; to every man according to his several ability; and straightway took his journey.*
>
> *Then he that had received the five talents went and traded with the same, and made them other five talents.*
>
> *And likewise he that had received two, he also gained other two.*
>
> *But he that had received one went and digged in the earth, and hid his lord's money.*
>
> *After a long time the lord of those servants cometh, and reckoneth with them.*

*And so he that had received five talents came and brought other five talents, saying, Lord, thou deliveredst unto me five talents: behold, I have gained beside them five talents more.*

*His lord said unto him, Well done, thou good and faithful servant: thou hast been faithful over a few things, I will make thee ruler over many things: enter thou into the joy of thy lord.*

*He also that had received two talents came and said, Lord, thou deliveredst unto me two talents: behold, I have gained two other talents beside them.*

*His lord said unto him, Well done, good and faithful servant; thou hast been faithful over a few things, I will make thee ruler over many things: enter thou into the joy of thy Lord.*

*Then he which had received the one talent came and said, Lord, I knew thee that thou art an hard man, reaping where thou hast not sown, and gathering where thou hast not strawed:*

*And I was afraid, and went and hid thy talent in the earth: lo, there thou hast that is thine.*

*His lord answered and said unto him, Thou wicked and slothful servant, thou knewest that l reap where I sowed not, and gather where I have not strawed:*

*Thou oughtest therefore to have put my money to the exchangers, and then at my coming I should have received mine own with usury.*

*Take therefore the talent from him, and give it unto him which hath ten talents.*

*For unto every one that hath shall be given, and he shall have abundance: but from him that hath not shall be taken away even that which he hath.*

> *And cast ye the unprofitable servant into outer darkness: there shall be weeping and gnashing of teeth* (Matthew 25:14-30).

Now, why did the Master react like this? Was it because the servant went out and lived with prostitutes? Was it because he lived a riotous life of drinking and gambling? Was he a liar or a thief? No. This man had already been chosen to be a servant of Christ. He was already called to be a member of the Kingdom of God, just like you and I. He was cast out of the Kingdom because he allowed his life in Christ to be controlled and dominated by one particular demon agent in Satan's army.

Yes, this man was literally vexed and tormented to such a degree that he needed deliverance. He was like so many people in the world today (even born-again Christians) who are useless to God and feel helpless to do anything about it.

Remember that this parable was Jesus's way of giving us a deep spiritual truth with which to warn us of a major spiritual pitfall. Earlier in the Gospel of Matthew, Jesus warns us that not everyone who cries, "Lord, Lord," is going to live with Him in heaven, but only he who does the will of the Father (see Matthew 7:21).

Yet, on that final day, this servant said (in essence) to the Master: "I was afraid. I went out and hid your talent in the ground. I hid the resources you gave me to save souls because I was ruled by fear. I could not do Your will because fear ruled my mind, my spirit, my emotions, and my actions. I was afraid."

Like you and me, this servant had everything he needed to do the will of God. He was called for the Kingdom and was fully equipped for what he had to do. He had been given the same ability, power, and relationship with God as the servants who were given two talents and five talents. But on that final day, he had nothing with which to meet the Master but a feeble excuse for not making his life count for God.

I do not know of another power that can render you as helpless and useless, that can tie your hands, bind your mind, control, vex, and torment your soul like the spirit of fear!

## Fear Is a Spirit!

The apostle Paul warned Timothy, *"For God hath not given us the spirit of fear; but of power, and of love, and of a sound mind"* (2 Timothy 1:7). The Word also tells us that, *"fear hath torment"* (1 John 4:18). Therefore, since fear is a tormenting spirit, we know that it does not come from God. And if it does not come from God, there is only one other source fear can come from, and that is from Satan!

It is the devil's goal to keep you oppressed by fear, to prevent you from doing the will of God, and to keep you from being used by God in the gifts of the Spirit. Fear is one way that Satan keeps us in bondage to self. When God gives you a gift of His Spirit to give to others, Satan uses fear to make you think: *This might not be God. It's probably just me, and I'll make a fool of myself. I'd better hold back.*

Fear is also the devil's tool to keep us in bondage to the opinions of man. We are afraid of what people will think or say about us. We become afraid that we might not be accepted in our denomination if we go all the way for God.

I know of nothing that binds, vexes, torments, and keeps us from doing God's will more than fear. When we attend a spiritual meeting, God moves upon our heart to give money to reach the lost. As soon as we get home, Satan attacks: *You can't give that amount. It's too much. You were just being emotional. What will happen if you get cancer or lose your job? You have so little money in the bank.* Fear strikes, and God is robbed. Satan has won the victory. The door is now open for the enemy to come in and hinder the glorious promises of God. The unholy spirit of fear takes control. The Kingdom suffers.

Remember that judgment begins in the house of God (see 1 Peter 4:17). If you go down to defeat because of giving in to the spirit of fear, what will you say when you stand before God?

Friend, if you have ever made a pledge to God and not fulfilled that vow, I urge you to do so before you go one step further. I don't want you to stand before the Master and hear what the unprofitable servant heard. Jesus told him, *"Depart from me,"* and he was cast into outer darkness (see Luke 13:27).

We are to be ruled by love for our Lord, never by fear! The Book of Ecclesiastes tells us:

> *When you vow a vow or make a pledge to God, do not put off paying it; for God has no pleasure in fools (those who witlessly mock Him). Pay what you vow.* [See Proverbs 20:25; Acts 5:4.] *It is better that you should not vow than that you should vow and not pay* [See Psalm 50:14; 66:13-14; 76:11.] (Ecclesiastes 5:4-5 AMP).

Let us each determine today to overcome all fear so that we might glorify God by triumphantly saying to Him, *"Praise waiteth for thee, O God, in Sion: and unto thee shall the vow be performed"* (Psalm 65:1).

Beloved, it's harvest time! This is not a fire drill! It's the real thing! Jesus is coming! Let us all get our house in order quickly and, using all of the resources at our disposal, move on to total victory in Him.

## Fear Rules God's Servants Today

This unprofitable servant was afraid to use the resources that God had given him to use. He refused to use the tools that God had given him to overcome his fear. However, as sad as this story sounds, it is nothing compared to what is going on with God's servants today. If you don't believe me, just read several of the hundreds of letters I receive from Christians each week—Christians whose lives are fruitless and in complete bondage to the spirit of fear.

One friend writes:

> Brother Morris, I have agoraphobia (an abnormal fear of public places). I've been saved over three years, but God hasn't healed me yet. Please pray that the Lord Jesus will heal me of this torment so that I can go out and speak of Him and get a job.

Now listen to the way Satan has another dear Christian so paralyzed by fear that she is totally useless in fulfilling God's will for her life. She pleads:

> Dear Brother Cerullo and Theresa, please help me. I can't cope with this three-year-old problem that seems to be getting worse. I really need help.
>
> Why is it that I have the most difficult time maintaining eye contact with anyone? On account of it, I fear people. I find it so difficult to fellowship with anyone. Even my relationship with my husband is shaky, and I have problems trying to communicate with my child.
>
> I don't have any friends. There are people who want my friendship, but it seems that I can't let them. I retreat from them with a sort of weird look in my eyes, and with a fearful and timid attitude.
>
> It's such a helpless feeling that overwhelms me. I almost have to force myself to go anywhere.
>
> I asked God not long ago to give me a burden for people so that I could reach out to them and give myself to them.
>
> Well, praise God, the burden is there, but the problem is that whenever there's a need for me to reach out, I panic. I get frightened and find it difficult to even face them.
>
> What is this? I know that God did not create me this way. There are people in need everywhere, and here I am, just wasting my life.

I hope your heart is breaking as you see the desperation in this life. These same fears may be yours. Yet God's Word commands that we must (and can) rise up and overcome all of our fears. Those who do not overcome fear will be cast into the lake of fire, right along with all of the other unprofitable agents of Satan.

> *But the fearful, and unbelieving, and the abominable, and murderers, and whoremongers, and sorcerers, and idolaters, and all liars, shall have their part in the lake which burneth with fire and brimstone: which is the second death* (Revelation 21:8).

I know this is not a passage that many of you have underlined in your Bible. Yet it is just as true as all of the promises for prosperity, health, and happiness that we're so fond of. Believe me, if God's Word says something, we have two choices: We can either take it very seriously, or we can fall into deceit. Which do you choose?

When you stand before your Lord on that final day, are you going to face Him with the many "treasures" of lost souls that you've won and nurtured, or with a lot of feeble excuses of why you were afraid to step out?

> *...For unto whomsoever much is given, of him shall much be required: and to whom men have committed much, of him they will ask the more* (Luke 12:48).

Are you going to say, "Yes, Lord. I obeyed Your every command. I took every tool You gave me, overcame my fears, and was victorious for You." Or are you going to say, "Well, I know Your Word said, 'Fear not,' but I didn't think that applied to me. You see, I had a burden to pray for the sick, but I was afraid to learn to drive, so I never got far from my house." Or, "I was the shy type, so I never got into witnessing. I did play the piano in Sunday school, though. Wasn't that enough?" Or, "I was afraid that if I tithed, I wouldn't have enough for myself. I was afraid to trust You to provide for me."

So what was the unprofitable servant's excuse for being afraid? Fear of poverty! He told the Lord:

> *Sir, I knew you were a hard man, and I was afraid you would rob me of what I earned, so I hid your money in the earth...* (Matthew 25:25 TLB).

What about you? Are you in bondage to the fear of giving because you're afraid that the Lord might ask you for more, or that the well will run dry?

Many of you are in such bondage to fear that you are afraid to receive healing from God. So many are like the little woman who came to me at a meeting in West Virginia, hobbling on two great big canes. I said to this lady, "In the Name of Jesus, drop those canes."

She said, "I can't do that."

I asked, "Why not?"

She said, "Because I'm afraid I will fall."

At that point I put my hand on her and cast out the spirit of fear, in the Name of Jesus. Then I grabbed those two canes and pulled them out from under her while her eyes were closed. Then I gave her a little push and said, "Now, get going." She had only two alternatives. One was to fall, and the other was to walk. She decided she would walk and was totally healed, but there are many who decide they will not.

I tell you, the Church today is being ruled by a spirit of fear. Because of this, hundreds of thousands of "born-again" Christians, who think they're in good shape with the Lord, are sinking fast into "unprofitable servanthood." This includes pastors, ministers, and evangelists. Yes, the spirit of fear is not only ruling the pews, it's in the pulpit too.

## DISCUSSION QUESTIONS

1. Do you personally know someone who struggles with persistent fears?
2. Can you think of an occasion when you acted (or did not act) based on a fear?
3. In what part of your life does the spirit of fear usually attack you?

CHAPTER 2

# MINISTERS ARE IN TORMENT

UNFORTUNATELY, WE LIVE IN AN age and in a society where the image we have of our local minister (or evangelist or teacher) is that of someone who is high on a pedestal, three miles removed from the anguish of the tormenting fears of Satan. The minister then feels a tremendous inner burden to live up to his stainless steel image. Tremendous energy drains out of his innermost being as he struggles day after day to "keep the mask on." Publicly, he usually succeeds.

But the turmoil raging inside his soul is another matter. There, he carries on more wars with fear and anxiety than most of us could ever deal with. One typical example is a pastor who recently wrote to me in desperation. He said:

> Brother Cerullo, we are a pastor family in a "holiness" denomination, and we are filled with the Spirit, but we are battling with the problem of being very double-minded. We are being tortured by Satan with fears, doubts, and fears of rejection—unable to stand firm.

> When God leads us to pray for the sick or to work miracles, we are beginning to take courage to do it. In many cases, while we are beginning to pray or move on it, fear hits us, and we are not able to complete the work.

This man is not alone. There is another fine pastor in Massachusetts (whom I love dearly) who is another example of how fear is robbing preachers (and their entire congregations) of the glory and power of God.

One day this man told me that he would be one of my main supporters if I held a meeting in his city. So I went to that city, and God gave us a great meeting. However, as I looked around for this pastor, I could not find him. God was shaking the place with His Presence, but this man (who had the largest Full Gospel church in the area) never showed up.

After I had been there several weeks, I got a phone call from him. He said, "Brother Cerullo, I would have been so happy to sponsor your revival."

I said, "Then why weren't you out?"

He answered, "Please pray for me. I would have been there if I could, but I couldn't. I'm afraid."

I asked, "Afraid of what?"

He replied, "I'm afraid of my deacon board."

He went on to tell me that just before I came to town they had started a radio broadcast. According to him, "We're beginning to get some nice people in the church. The deacons were afraid that if the folks knew we were connected with a meeting like yours, we might lose them. We carry on such a big program that we can't afford to have anything happen."

I said, "Brother, how many people did you get out for your Sunday night service?"

He murmured, "About forty or fifty."

Where was the rest of the town? They were at our meeting! All of those people that his deacons were so worried about scaring away were at our place, some of them until 2 a.m., getting the Baptism of the Holy Ghost!

Oh, how the fear of man is keeping hundreds of thousands of people and their pastors not only away from the blessings of God, but away from obeying Jesus and moving out in the power of God! Pastors are afraid of their congregations. Congregations are afraid of their pastors. Pastors are afraid of each other, afraid that the church down the street might get a few more tithe-paying sheep. I can just hear the agonizing cry of our Lord as He warns and pleads with us:

> *My friends, do not be afraid of those who kill the body and after that have no more that they can do. But I will warn you whom to fear: fear the One who, after He has killed, has authority to cast into hell; yes, I tell you, fear Him!* (Luke 12:4-5 NASB)

A few years ago another pastor confided, "I really don't want to teach spiritual warfare. Talking about Satan might scare people." But, praise God, this man got the victory over the fears in his own life and today is raising up one of the most powerful youth armies for God in the country! His congregation has more than doubled.

Right now, God is looking for thousands of pastors, ministers, and evangelists like this man. Before Christ returns, He is going to purge His Body of all of the dead works that we've been locked into because of fear, all of the cold, joyless formalism which holds congregations in bondage because their pastors are afraid of the Spirit of God.

## The Flesh or the Spirit?

How my heart grieves to see so many of you, who long to sing, to testify, and to move out in the gifts of the Holy Spirit, hold back because you're afraid you will say the wrong thing. You hold words of life "in your hands," and are afraid to deliver them! There are whole congregations who are terrified to lift up their hands to the Lord or to issue a prayer request at a small gathering. Of course, giving a prophecy or a message in tongues is out of the question!

So many people long to see the gifts of the Holy Spirit in operation (the gifts that God gave to us to build and equip His Church), but the pastors are so afraid of their people "getting in the flesh" that they never get in the Spirit.

One man started to get the Baptism of the Holy Ghost in my meeting. He began to speak in other tongues. Then, all of a sudden, he stopped. I asked him, "Why did you stop after you started to speak?"

He answered, "When I started speaking, it sounded like I myself was speaking. I got to thinking that it was me and not God, and I became afraid."

You do not have to be afraid. God, your Father, will not give you something that isn't of Him (see Luke 11:11,13). Do not be afraid to "let go." The Word of God commands us:

> *Never lag in zeal and in earnest endeavor; be aglow and burning with the Spirit, serving the Lord* (Romans 12:11 AMP).

God literally dwells in the praises of His people (see Psalms 22:3). You need never be afraid to use all of the talents that He Himself has put within you to enable you to worship Him in spirit and in truth. You do not have to fear anybody else's opinion when He gives you a Word which will heal or encourage one of His suffering lambs. You need only to stand up and give it! If you insist on living in the fear of being emotional or of being "in the flesh," you will never know what it is like to be used of God in the Spirit.

But you say, "Wait a minute, Brother Cerullo, I'm not one of those people who is bound by fear. I'm fine."

You are? Then let me ask you, how many souls have you won to Christ during the past twelve months? How about in the last six months? Three months? How many unpaid vows do you have? How often have you used your talents to proclaim God's Word to the lost? To heal the sick? To bind up someone who is broken-hearted? To set one of Satan's captives free? What kind of excuse are you going to present to the Master?

Jesus has ordained that:

> *But ye shall receive power, after that the Holy Ghost is come upon you: and ye shall be witnesses unto me both in Jerusalem, and in all Judaea, and in Samaria, and unto the uttermost part of the earth* (Acts 1:8).

Satan is keeping many of you so bound by fear that you can't even witness to your neighbor or fellow worker at your job.

The strongest satanic deception in the Church today is that Satan's demons operate only outside the Body of Christ, and that when it comes to Christians, these demons have no real power. Meanwhile, the demonic spirit of fear is keeping a majority of God's people tied up in fruitless bondage, deceived into thinking that it's all right to sit back and wait for heaven—when, in reality, they are headed for "outer darkness."

All of this directly relates to Satan's second most destructive deception.

## YOUR FEAR AFFECTS OTHERS

One of the most destructive deceptions from Satan is that your fear affects you alone. There are literally thousands of different fears that bind the Church today. Every day we face the fear of cats, trees, cars, airplanes, being alone, being rejected, being around people, intimacy, relationships, responsibility, commitment, poverty, success, losing what you have, the opinions of others, and impending sicknesses. But the one deception that Satan has succeeded in pulling off in the minds of all of those who fear, is that failure to overcome your little fear is no big deal because it affects you and you alone.

Let me tell you something. No fear that you hang onto or fail to get the victory over ever affects only you alone! We are all one in the Spirit, and any fear which hinders you ultimately has a devastating effect on the whole Body of Christ in the spirit world.

This is why God has always refused to allow the fearful to remain in His Army! In essence He told them: Go home. We don't want you. We don't need you. When we go to war you'll only contaminate the others. (See Deuteronomy 20:8 and Judges 7:3.)

In God's Army today it doesn't matter what your fear is. The truth is that all fear emanates from a demonic spirit of fear who has gained a foothold in your mind and is an archenemy of God. If this spirit of fear is allowed to retain its foothold, sooner or later it will rise up to hinder, block, and prevent Christ's life from flowing through you when you need it the most.

Friend, are you ready to do something about it?

In many ways God's army today is like the children of Israel were when they came out of Egypt. After they were delivered, what was the first thing they were faced with? The Red Sea! What was their reaction to it? They were paralyzed with fear! Fear literally overtook their minds as they turned against Moses, complaining:

> *...Have you brought us out here to die in the desert because there were not enough graves for us in Egypt?* (Exodus 14:11 TLB)

At first, Moses desperately tried to encourage them by telling them to hang in there. "Just stand still," he said. "The Lord will fight for you." But at that point the Lord Himself broke in with a direct command: *"Quit praying and get the people moving! Forward, march!"* (Exodus 14:15 TLB).

These are the same orders our Commander is giving us now. He is telling us that it's time to quit whining about our fears and time to get moving in our offensive warfare against the devil. Therefore, as of today, you and I are going to go after every demonic power of fear that is binding your life and destroying your witness for Christ!

You say, "Brother Cerullo, you sound angry."

I am angry—not at you, but at Satan for robbing you of Christ's riches in this life and of your reward in His Kingdom to come! We are going to stop this now! We are going to rip the mask right off of the devil and his tactics, openly and without fear.

I have exposed his strategies and am providing you with a foundation for conquering him in every aspect of your life. You are not going to hide. You are not going to remain on the defensive. You are not fighting a war of preservation.

God's Word has already told us why He sent His Son to deliver us. It was:

> *That he would grant unto us, that we being delivered out of the hand of our enemies might serve him without fear. In holiness and righteousness before him, all the days of our life* (Luke 1:74-75).

Bless God, you have heard His battle cry against fear in your heart. You are now going to come down out of your high tower of intellectual knowledge and move out onto the battlefield. All of the joy, courage, confidence, peace, vitality, and zeal that Satan has stolen from you through fear will be restored to you in the mighty Name of Jesus.

> *For God hath not given us the spirit of fear; but of power, and of love, and of a sound mind* (2 Timothy 1:7).

Get ready. You are about to begin a victorious life!

## Discussion Questions

1. Have you ever felt like God was prompting you to do something, but you held back because you weren't sure if you were imagining it?
2. Who in your life might be affected by your fears?
3. Ministers are often burdened by fear of losing support. Can you think of ways to support a minister, pastor, or spiritual leader in your life?

CHAPTER 3

# CAN A CHRISTIAN BE DEMON-POSSESSED?

BEFORE WE EXPLORE THE KEYS to overcoming fear, I'd like to answer one question with which I'm sure many of you are eager to challenge me. That is, "Brother Cerullo, are you telling me that a born-again Christian can be demon-possessed?"

The answer is no, at least not in the way that we usually think of "possession." Let me explain.

First of all, there is no distinction in the Bible between oppression, possession, vexation, or anything else that demons can do to you. The word used in the New Testament for anyone suffering from demonic pressure was *daimonizomai*. The modern interpretation of this word would be "demonized."

To further understand what it means to be demonized, you might ask: "What kind of spirit is in control of (or ruling) my life any time I react in great fear?" For instance, if you suddenly turn pale, go into a cold sweat, tremble, and start screaming when you become frightened, what kind of spirit would you say is in control of your mind at that moment—the Spirit of God or the spirit of fear? If you become violently ill when you even think about getting on an airplane, which spirit is ruling your mind at that time? I'll tell you, it sure isn't the Spirit of God.

Then where is God when all of this is happening? You *know* that you've accepted Jesus as your personal Savior. You know that you have received His Holy Spirit. If this is so, then where is He when these vicious fears strike?

Beloved, your Lord has promised that He will never leave you nor forsake you (see Hebrews 13:5). Therefore, He is right there all the time, standing by in your new inner self.

You say, "Why is He 'standing by,' Brother Cerullo? Why doesn't He do something?"

Believe me, He wants to, if you will only learn how to let Him. He is waiting for you to call on Him in those moments of hidden terror. He is waiting for you to learn to recognize His Presence within you and to tap into His power so that He might rise up from within you and defeat the enemy.

## Christ's Life Within You Can Never Be Possessed

You see, that perfect seed of Christ's life, which was planted within you when you were born again, can never be possessed, oppressed, or in any way infiltrated by the enemy. It is impregnable, incapable of being assaulted or penetrated by any outside, evil force.

However, that precious seed of Christ's life in your inner man is like a tiny embryo encased by the outer "shell" of your old nature. During your years of spiritual growth, this outer shell will begin to crack, crumble, and eventually fall away as the "new person" within you starts to grow and emerge. This process is much like a baby chick coming out of its shell. Step by step the chick becomes stronger and stronger as it pecks its way out, until one day it totally breaks through to the outside world.

Through all of this, the chick is being mightily strengthened from within by having to break through its shell. By the time the chick does break through its shell, it is strong enough to cope with its new world. Likewise, you, too, are emerging as a totally new person in Christ. The Word of God assures you:

> *Therefore if any man be in Christ, he is a new creature: old things are passed away; behold, all things are become new* (2 Corinthians 5:17).

You say, "But Brother Cerullo, this verse says that old things (like my old fears) have passed away. Then why do I still have them?"

One biblical truth you will come to discover is that no promises in the Bible are simply dumped into our lap. From cover to cover, the Word of God is about pressing through to (and for) God. It is a Book about laboring and overcoming through Christ.

The children of Israel found this out the hard way. From the days of Abraham, God had allotted the Promised Land to them. Yet isn't it strange that they couldn't just walk into it after years in the wilderness, kick up their feet, and say, "Oh, Hallelujah! God gave us this land, and it's ours. We'll just settle down." Why couldn't they do this? Because the Promised Land was filled with enemies, and brother, they had to fight a battle to take every inch of the promise.

It's the same with our soul. Jesus has already paid the price to redeem it, but by the time you were born again, that mind of yours was infested with every kind of fear, negative thought pattern, rotten attitude, and worldly reasoning that the devil could pack into it.

So just as Canaan wasn't automatically purged of the resident enemies when the Israelites walked in, all of your fears didn't get automatically washed from your mind the day you said, "I love You, Jesus." What did happen when you were born again was that you were cleansed from the guilt of all of your sins and fears. You were not automatically freed from the power of sin or the power of fear. That is why there is a spiritual war raging in your life right now:

> *For we wrestle not against flesh and blood, but against principalities, against powers, against the rulers of the darkness of this world, against spiritual wickedness in high places* (Ephesians 6:12).

## THE CHALLENGE OF SPIRITUAL GROWTH

Jesus Christ is coming back for a bride without spot or wrinkle (see Ephesians 5:27). When you came to Him, you were not without spot or wrinkle. Your mind and soul were a mess. This is the reason you must fight to reclaim the territory of your mind by overcoming a foe who has already been defeated.

Yes, Satan was defeated by Jesus. Through the power of Christ in us, we too must conquer him. Through our Lord Jesus Christ, God has given to you all of the authority, the ability, and the power to become perfect in Him. He has given you all that you need to lay hold of Christ's victory and be more than conquerors (see Romans 8:37). You have been fully equipped with everything necessary to grow up into the mature, perfect Bride for His Son.

Obviously, Satan does not want you to use what God has given you. He wants to keep you in bondage to him (through fear), so that you never become an acceptable Bride. The only way Satan can do this is to find a foothold in your unrenewed mind, to "roar" at you with fearful thoughts, and hope you will accept them. The worst thing you can do when this happens is to run back into your shell or give in to these fears.

However, God has no intention of letting you give in or go down to defeat. He intends for you to emerge strong and triumphant. God says:

> *...And if he draws back and shrinks in fear, My soul has no delight or pleasure in him.* [See Habakkuk 2:3-4.] *But our way is not that of those who draw back to eternal misery... but we are of those who believe [who cleave to and trust in and rely on God through Jesus Christ, the Messiah] and by faith preserve the soul* (Hebrews 10:38-39 AMP).

I will warn you now that Satan will try to latch onto every fear you have ever had in the past in an effort to press in and strangle that new spiritual life within you. His goal is to see that you never reach spiritual maturity.

Don't be afraid! Think of Satan's demonic spirit of fear as a big, black baboon that is trying to hang onto the "cage" of your old, unrenewed self. There he is, rattling it, shaking it, screeching at you, trying with all of his might to get you to shrink back in fear and stifle that tiny light inside. His aim is to so thoroughly possess your old nature that the new person within you never has a chance. You must resist! This is why spiritual growth is not easy.

The apostle Paul himself said, *"My little children, of whom I travail in birth again until Christ be formed in you"* (Galatians 4:19). As Paul found out, getting people "saved" was the easy part. Getting them to grow up to be spiritually mature and victorious was a different matter. It is not automatic. The apostle John reinforces this when he tells us, *"But as many as received him, to them gave he power to become the sons of God..."* (John 1:12).

Some don't make it. Five (50 percent) of the ten virgins who went out to meet the bridegroom (Jesus) were shut out of the wedding feast (see Matthew 25:1-10). Can you imagine a 50 percent fatality rate in the Church today?

I can.

Why? Because of fear.

So, are you ready to do something about all of those treacherous fears that are haunting your life? If you are, then let's get started.

## Fear Is a Creative Force

The first step to overcoming any problem is to understand it. In our case, we must fully understand that the spirit of fear is actually a powerful force for evil which can create or call into being the very thing that is feared. Job experienced this when he said:

> *For the thing which I greatly feared is come upon me, and that which I was afraid of is come unto me* (Job 3:25).

This being so, how does evil power work?

Ever since God created the universe, spiritual powers have had dominion over mental powers, and the powers of the mind have had dominion over the physical realm.

Therefore, whatever spirits we choose to accept into our mind will determine what will be manifested in our physical realm. For example, if you choose to allow the spirit of fear in your life, you will think fearful thoughts, speak fearful words, and what you fear will eventually come to pass. If you choose to accept God's spirit of peace, then you will think peaceful thoughts, speak in peace, and create serenity all around you.

Make no mistake. There are only two kinds of spiritual forces in the world—those that are of God (for good) and those that are of Satan (for evil). You have the Spirit above all spirits (the Spirit of God) dwelling deep in your innermost being. The crucial question you must still face daily is, which spirit—the Spirit of God or the spirit of fear—will I choose to accept into my mind today? Which thoughts will I accept or reject?

Be warned that whichever side you permit to control your thoughts, that side will control your entire being.

> *Know ye not, that to whom ye yield yourselves servants to obey, his servants ye are to whom ye obey; whether of sin to death, or of obedience unto righteousness?* (Romans 6:16)

## Fear Is a Fact, but Fear Is an Act

I have often taught that faith is a fact, but faith is also an act. What I have meant is that faith, as a creative spiritual force, is not manifested in the physical realm until you choose with your mind and your will to bring it into being by acting on it.

Fear works the same way. Satan can roar at you all he wants to, but if you refuse to let his fearful thoughts dwell in your mind and refuse to act on them, there's nothing more he can do. He will flee from your resistance!

However, if you choose to act on the suggestions planted by the spirit of fear (or use the words of your mouth to reinforce them), you have released a powerful evil force to start working. What's more, acting and reacting to fear soon becomes a dangerous habit which is very hard to break.

This is why in the Garden of Eden, Satan wasted no time in going after Eve's mind. He knew that if she accepted his suggestions in her mind, these thoughts would then feed her will. Once she chose (with her will) to act on them, she was his.

## Discussion Questions

1. Have you ever experienced a fear or worry becoming reality in your life?
2. Have you ever had something positive happen that you hoped for and had faith for?
3. How can you cultivate the influence of God's Spirit in your life while rejecting the roots of fear?

CHAPTER 4

# THE INVISIBLE WAR FOR YOUR MIND

IN THE INVISIBLE, SPIRITUAL WAR for our mind, we will see how the spirit of fear leads us directly into unbelief. Unbelief prevents the promises of God from being received in your life. By studying Satan's operations, we can see that all fear is based on his success in planting seeds of deception in our mind (particularly in our imagination) and getting us to act on them.

In the Church today we hear so much about faith and living the life of faith. Do you know why most people can't exercise true faith? Because they don't have their mind and their imagination under control.

The Bible says that, *"faith is the substance of things hoped for, the evidence of things not seen"* (Hebrews 11:1). When you hope for something, you know exactly what you are hoping for because you picture it in your mind. What you visualize actually shapes what you will become (see Proverbs 23:7). Therefore, faith is the manifestation (or the evidence) of whatever mental pictures you build up in your mind.

Yet many of you are living in such a state of defeat in your minds that you can't imagine that you really are the overcomer that God says you are! You can't imagine that you have total victory over the fears within you. You can't even imagine how you would act if you were fearless.

You do not have the mental picture of yourself that God wants you to have, based on His Word. Instead of seeing yourself as a new person in Christ (fully trusting Him to empower you to overcome), you see only the negative things that dominated your old nature. You are possessed with the past. In your mind's eye you see a whole life of failures based on fears—fears that keep cropping up in your imagination as you yield to them and feed on them.

I don't believe there's a person reading this book who hasn't been attacked by fear in their imagination. For example, from earliest childhood we are programmed by the devil to expect (see ourselves in) poor health in our old age. In our imagination we just know that we will end up with arthritis. We expect our joints to tighten up, our mind to get dull, and our hearing to go bad.

People are constantly telling me, "This illness runs in my family. My father had this pain all his life, and now I've got it. I always knew I'd get it." Where do they get such vain imaginations? Not from the Spirit of God! They are all fueled by fear.

This is why the Spirit of God specifically told Paul that we must rise up and cast down every vain, foul imagination that comes against us (see 2 Corinthians 10:5). Our imagination is the first stronghold that we must bring under control if we are to thoroughly conquer fear.

Did you know that most people who commit adultery picture it first? Sin first comes as a thought in our imagination. It is the same with fear. Fear first comes as a thought from the enemy. If we refuse to rebuke it, then suddenly we're ruled by it. To illustrate this, let's look at a typical example of how this is working in the Church.

## Fear Attack

Imagine that you have joined a new fellowship and are eager to begin its Wednesday night Bible studies. When that first Wednesday night rolls around, it's cold and rainy outside. The spirit of fear taunts your mind and says, *You'd better not go out tonight. The weather is miserable, and you're going to get sick.*

You accept this thought and help it along in your imagination. *That's right,* you say to yourself. *I always get sick if I go out when it's like this. If I get a cold this time, I know I'll get pneumonia. I'd better play it safe and stay home just this once.*

So you act on the enemy's seed of fear and stay home. Granted, you do not get a cold, but something dangerous and deceptive has happened. You are now convinced that you remained healthy not because God protected you, but because you stayed home out of the rain!

The next Wednesday night is also chilly and rainy, so you stay home again, unfruitful for God because you're locked into the fear of getting a cold. You have begun to form a habit of obeying the fear instead of obeying God. As the apostle Peter warns us: "*...for of whom a man is overcome, of the same is he brought in bondage*" (2 Peter 2:19).

You have become a slave to fear. Then one day someone tells you that God would be much more pleased if you would act in faith and get out to that Bible study, rain or no rain. But by now you're even afraid to drive in the rain. Satan has progressed to the next stage of drawing you into bondage, for by now you just can't believe that God would see you through. From this, we can see that all fear is the first step to unbelief.

It is shocking to see how this is exactly the same process which Satan successfully pulled off in the minds of the children of Israel, the same tactics which caused them to fail to enter into the Promised Land of God. Let's see what took place.

In the Book of Numbers, we read how, after years of wandering in the desert, the children of Israel were finally at the gates of the Promised Land. All they had to do was to believe God's Word, trust Him, and enter in. However, they decided to send twelve spies into the territory to check things out first. What happened?

Ten out of the twelve spies disobeyed God by taking their eyes off of Him and His promises and putting them on their enemies instead. Seeing this, Satan immediately went to work on their minds. By the time the ten stood up to give their report to the people, the spirit of fear had total control of their imaginations. Instead of expressing faith in God, they could only rebel in unbelief and wail:

> *...The land, through which we have gone to search it, is a land that eateth up the inhabitants thereof; and all the people that we saw in it are men of a great stature. And there we saw the giants...and we were in our own sight as grasshoppers, and so we were in their sight* (Numbers 13:32-33).

From this, we learn a very important lesson. That is, Satan's end objective is not merely to keep you in bondage to fear but to lull you into a state of unbelief through that fear. And unbelief always leads to rebellion against God's Word!

Remember, although Satan had successfully instilled fears in the minds of the children of Israel, God did not ban them from the Promised Land because their imaginations had gone wild. What really hammered the nails into their coffins was the fact that after they had surrendered to fear, "*...they could not enter in because of unbelief*" (Hebrews 3:19).

Right now, I beg you to realize that your "little fears" are far more dangerous in the long run than you may suspect. Ultimately, each one of them will lead to unbelief and a dangerous denial of God and His Word, which is considered (in His eyes) rebellion. Please, I beg you to face this question today: *Who has control of my thoughts and my imagination, Satan or God?*

## DON'T LOOK BACK!

Unfortunately, what happened to the children of Israel was no isolated incident. I see Satan's same fear tactics take root in the imaginations of countless Christians day after day.

Just last week a beautiful young lady said, "Please pray for my mother. She had cancer a number of years ago and she just knows it's coming back now."

I asked, "Has she been to a doctor?"

She replied, "No. She's too depressed to go out because she just knows that it's going to get her this time."

How tragic. Here is a talented woman living a life of secret terror, closed up in her house, bound in torment because Satan has convinced her that all she can do is get ready to die.

Next, he moves in with self-condemnation, guilt, and bitterness. Self-hate and resentment follow, all close companions of fear. You see, the spirit of fear usually does not work alone. Satan's armies are highly organized, and evil spirits cooperate closely with one another to maintain control of the mind.

Thus, a foothold of fear becomes part of a stronghold—a stronghold housing guilt, isolation, unforgiveness, confusion, and more fear. The torment accelerates as the victim cries, "What's wrong with me? Why hasn't God delivered me?"

Well, what *is* wrong?

One friend pinpointed the problem precisely when she said, "I don't know why I'm afraid, but I've *always* been afraid."

That's it exactly. All fears are based on the past. All fears depend on you looking back to something that happened to you in the past, even if it was only an hour ago.

Jesus said, *"...if therefore thine eye be single, thy whole body shall be full of light"* (Matthew 6:22). There is no way that any fear can hover in the dark recesses of your mind when your eye is single-mindedly set on your Lord and His Word. You're afraid today because you have your eyes glued to the wrong place. You are being ruled by what has been.

Think about it. Pinpoint your own fears. When did you first experience them? In childhood? After an auto accident? When your parents were divorced? The first time a door was slammed in your face? Whatever it was, that incident (or incidents) was a point of entry for Satan to plant seeds of guilt and fear in your old nature, and you got stuck there. You began to talk yourself into believing that all of the pain and fears of the past were still real. You kept them alive through your self-talk.

Make no mistake. Words are powerful. Even the silent words that you "speak" in conversations with yourself have a dramatic effect on your entire being. Through your self-talk you can literally talk yourself into cooperating with the spirit of fear, and remain in bondage to it. "If I get close to anybody, they'll only use me, so I'd better keep my distance," you say. So, you never get close to anyone, not even God.

"I'll never get married. I can't stand all of the fighting."

"I hate religion. When I was a kid, my folks dragged me to church. I'll never go again."

"I'll never be able to give. We've always been poor."

What you are really saying through all of this is, "I really don't believe I'm a new creation in Christ Jesus. I'm afraid to let go. I'm afraid to fully surrender myself to the Lord. I'm afraid to trust Him to remold my life. I'll just stay the way I am."

Stop telling yourself these things! The Word of God is commanding you:

> *Forget the former things; do not dwell on the past. See, I am doing a new thing! Now it springs up; do you not perceive it?* (Isaiah 43:18-19 NIV)

## Put Off the Old Man

When God first informed Jeremiah that he was called to be a prophet, the boy's first reaction was fear. "*...Ah, Lord God! behold, I cannot speak: for I am a child*" (Jeremiah 1:6). God immediately admonished him:

> *...Say not, I am a child: for thou shalt go to all that I shall send thee.... Be not afraid of their faces: for I am with thee*

> *to deliver thee...therefore gird up thy loins, and arise...be not dismayed at their faces...For, behold, I have made thee this day a defenced city, and an iron pillar, and brasen walls against the whole land. And they shall fight against thee; but they shall not prevail against thee; for I am with thee, saith the Lord, to deliver thee* (Jeremiah 1:7-8,17-19).

Notice that the first thing God corrected with Jeremiah was his self-talk, telling him, *"Say not."* Then He went after the image that Jeremiah had of himself, changing it from the fearful one that Jeremiah had clung to (based on what he was in the past), to the one that God was shaping for him in the present. God had great things in store for Jeremiah, but Jeremiah had to face his fears and get rid of his past image first, starting with his thoughts and the way he talked to himself.

Right now the Word of God promises you that, *"whatsoever thou shalt bind on earth shall be bound in heaven"* (Matthew 16:19). This includes all of those poisonous thoughts that fuel the spirit of fear! As of today, start binding and casting out those demonically-inspired thoughts from your mind. Today is a new day. You are a new creation, and God is commanding you:

> *Strip yourselves of your former nature [put off and discard your old unrenewed self].... And be constantly renewed in the spirit of your mind [having a fresh mental and spiritual attitude], and put on the new nature...created in God's image...* (Ephesians 4:22-24 AMP).

Believe me, God would not command you to do something if you could not do it.

The Spirit of God is telling you: *"Fear not. Cut the shorelines of your past. A new day is breaking forth upon you. Even now, press through into that which you have spoken unto Me, that which is your heart's desire. Be free from fear. Step out into My love, and you will not sink. You will see My power and My faithfulness in cutting loose those things which have held you in bondage to fear. Release yourself into a new dependence upon Me."*

You are ready to press on past the past. From now on, you're going to be able to draw a line and separate the thoughts of your "old self" of the past from the things the Spirit of God is telling your new self. This does not mean that all of the fears associated with your past will never come up before you again. It does mean that when they do, you are not going to wait five seconds before you successfully deal with them. How? Read on.

You are about to enter a new dimension of spiritual strength, a new strength that you have never experienced before. You are about to become an overcomer!

## Discussion Questions

1. Have you ever experienced "history repeating itself"? Were you worrying beforehand that it would happen that way?
2. Do you have any bad past experiences you just haven't been able to put behind you?
3. What positive hopes for the future can you replace those past experiences with? Start reciting them to yourself today.

## CHAPTER 5

# THE SECRET OF SPIRITUAL STRENGTH

AT THIS POINT, I KNOW that you have a deep desire to be freed from every one of your fears. But by now you are also aware that if you are ever going to gain victory over fear, there's going to be a fight! Spiritual battles take energy—energy which you don't think you have right now.

I can just hear you moaning, "Brother Cerullo, where am I ever going to get the strength to fight? The devil has me so wrung out, I don't have one ounce of energy left."

I know you don't. So I'm now going to show you the reason why you have not been able to press through to victory in your battles against fear. It is because it takes spiritual energy to stand and fight. Spiritual battles cannot be fought in natural strength. Inside, your spiritual well has run dry. Therefore, you've fallen into the habit of retreating or compromising in defeat.

This is what is called a defensive position in warfare. A defensive position doesn't take any energy at all; an offensive position does. You have been too bound by fear to get in touch with God's power within you and fight offensively.

So how do you tap into His abundant energy? There is only one secret to real spiritual strength.

## THE TRUTH HIMSELF SHALL MAKE YOU FREE

In the Bible, God promises us that, *"...If ye continue in my word, then are ye my disciples indeed; and ye shall know the truth, and the truth shall make you free"* (John 8:31-32). Notice that in the first half of His instructions, God establishes a prerequisite for freedom. That prerequisite is, "if you abide in My Word." In other words, if you do your part by living in total obedience to His Word, then you shall know the truth, and within the truth itself is all the strength and power you need to be fully free.

So the first question I want to ask you is: "Are you abiding daily in His Word?" Next, let me ask you: "If it is the truth itself which makes us free, what is the truth?"

Somebody said to me, "The truth is the Word of God."

That is correct, but the Word of God is more than just a written Book. The Word is also the living Word—who is Jesus Christ Himself! *"In the beginning was the Word, and the Word was with God, and the Word was God"* (John 1:1).

The Living Word, Jesus, is Himself the living Truth. He said, *"I am the way, the truth, and the life..."* (John 14:6). Therefore, it is the combination of your knowledge of the written Word, combined with your knowledge of the living Word and the living Truth (Jesus Christ) dwelling within you, which is the Source of all spiritual strength!

For years, many of you have been faithfully building a good spiritual foundation through your knowledge of the written Word. You know all about God's plan of salvation, His Great Commission, the keys of binding and loosing, the "Four Spiritual Laws," and everything else.

But those of you who have been paralyzed by fear have not built an equally firm foundation of personal knowledge and the personal experience of Him living within you. Your relationship with Him has been weak; therefore, your spiritual strength has also been weak. Because you have not been in touch daily with the experience of Christ within you, you have not been free.

You may know a lot about Him through His written Word, but if you don't know Him personally, your spiritual "house" will eventually crumble. He Himself warns, *"...without me ye can do nothing"* (John 15:5). The Pharisees of Jesus's day had to face this same issue when Jesus told them:

> *You search and investigate and pore over the Scriptures diligently, because you suppose and trust that you have eternal life through them. And these [very Scriptures] testify about Me! And still you are not willing [but refuse] to come to Me, so that you might have life* (John 5:39-40 AMP).

Freedom from fear takes spiritual strength, the kind of strength that can only be drawn from getting in touch with Christ in you, your hope of glory! (See Colossians 1:27.) In the most famous chapter on spiritual warfare ever written, the apostle Paul says:

> *In conclusion, be strong in the Lord [be empowered through your union with Him]; draw your strength from Him [that strength which His boundless might provides]* (Ephesians 6:10 AMP).

Remember that five of the ten ladies in Matthew 25 did not have the spiritual strength to make it to the wedding feast. Their lamps had run dry. Why? Until they actually stood face to face with the Lord, they had assumed they were in good shape. Instead, they were cast out. Why didn't they have the strength to make it in the end?

The Lord gave them the answer. He said, *"...I know you not"* (Matthew 25:12). Obviously, they knew His written Word, and they had gone out to meet Him. *But they had not spent their lives getting to know Him.* The most precious talent He gives us is our *time,* and they had not invested it wisely!

I beg you to be aware that it is only through a powerful, personal union with Him that you will ever come to know the true Source of spiritual strength. He is about to give you a breakthrough into the true knowledge of Him, which is the basis of that union. It is a union of strength. It is the union of His love.

## Break Through to Power over Fear

Several years ago, God revealed to me that all truth is parallel. By this, I mean that man lives in two worlds—the natural realm and the spiritual realm. Nothing happens in one world that doesn't have a parallel effect in the other. In our natural world we are seeing astounding things take place daily. Breakthroughs in science and technology that were considered science fiction only 50 years ago are now becoming commonplace.

What is a breakthrough? A breakthrough is a sudden burst of advanced knowledge. It is that sudden burst of revelation where, with a surge of insight, you suddenly look up and say, "I've got it!"

But if all truth is parallel, and these things are happening in the natural world, what is going on in the spiritual world and in the lives of born-again Christians? I'll tell you. Right now, God is pouring out His Spirit in a new work of grace and total restoration, deep in your inner self. He is taking you into a new spiritual dimension of revelation.

"Revelation of what, Brother Cerullo?"

The revelation of His Son in you! Remember that our definition of revelation has been "the drawing away of the veil of darkness." Until now you have been in darkness concerning His life, His love, and His power within you. God is about to give you a breakthrough into the true knowledge of Him dwelling in your heart.

Believe me, revelation is power! You will learn to both recognize and break through to His Presence within you. Empowered by His love, you will rise up in a new spirit of victory that will cause all fear to flee.

You say, "Brother Cerullo, what do you mean by a new work of restoration and grace?"

Let me explain. Throughout the Bible, God has always had two ways of doing things. The first way has been to work from outside His people, bestowing His blessings upon them—in other words, to do things for them. The second way has been to work in and through them from the inside out.

As an illustration, look at His plan of salvation. Salvation itself is a two-fold process. First is the work of salvation which Christ accomplished for us through His life, death, and resurrection. Second is the work that God wants to do within us through His Holy Spirit, empowering us from the inside out. The first part of salvation is the outward work of God, done for us. The second is His inward work, done within us.

For too long, people in the Church have been stuck in a rut, devoid of inner power, because they have been focusing all of their attention on what they wanted God to do *for* them and ignoring the powerful work that He longs to do *in* them. Thousands of people have come crying to the altar: "Oh, God, I can't get deliverance. Give me the victory over fear."

But God is telling them, "I put My Son, Jesus, inside you." *"...Greater is he that is in you, than he that is in the world"* (1 John 4:4). Stand up on your feet. Call on God. Fix your faith on Him. Let go of those fears, and let Him rise up against them. Let Him expel them from the inside out. When you do, you will never be the same.

## THE POWER OF GRACE

For years I've been saying that it's time for the Church to move beyond the point of blessing (what God wants to do for you) into the realm of power (what He wants to do within you). This is what I've been talking about. Right now, God wants you to have a breakthrough whereby you stop viewing His grace as simply an outward blessing or favor and come into the experience of it as the power of Christ within you, the only power that can overcome all fear.

If you have any doubts about God's grace as an actual power or spiritual force within you, listen to what our Lord told the apostle Paul about the famous thorn in his life. Three times Paul had asked the Lord to remove it (to do all the work for him from the outside). But the Lord told him, "*...My grace is sufficient for thee: for my strength is made perfect in weakness...*" (2 Corinthians 12:9).

Believe me, the Lord was not referring to His grace as some type of passive blessing. He was referring to it as a formidable inward force. It is His assistance within us which, when exercised by Paul, would strengthen him until the apostle—in union with the Lord—could overcome any foe!

This is the very force that God Himself is placing within you now to give you all of the breakthrough power you need to completely defeat fear.

> *For sin shall not [any longer] exert dominion over you, since now you are not under Law [as slaves], but under grace...* (Romans 6:14 AMP).

With God's new work of revelation and His new outpouring of grace in your heart, you will now have all of the assistance you need in your inner man to be dead to all fears and alive only to Christ. You will begin to discover for yourself, "*nevertheless I live; yet not I, but Christ liveth in me*" (Galatians 2:20). His astounding love for you will soon begin to break through all of the walls you have built out of fear. It will soon penetrate and rule all of your thoughts.

This is what it means to be renewed in the spirit of your mind (see Ephesians 4:23). All spirits of fear and darkness will be cast out, and the Spirit of God will be in, ruling all you do.

You ask, "When will all of this start taking place in my life?" It will start the moment you agree to stand on your feet and begin saying no to the spirit of fear! That is why this is an important growth period for you. It is a time when you will finally begin to:

> *Brace up and reinvigorate and set right your slackened and weakened and drooping hands and strengthen your feeble and palsied and tottering knees,* [Isaiah 35:3] *and cut through*

> *and make firm...straight paths for your feet...* (Hebrews 12:12-13 AMP).

This is also a time when our Lord is asking us to, "*...be on the watch to look [after one another], to see that no one falls back from and fails to secure God's grace...*" (Hebrews 12:15 AMP). Beloved, once you have begun to stand up and lay hold of God's grace within you, there is one more aspect of your personal relationship with Him that you must understand if you are to maintain total victory over fear.

## Discussion Questions

1. When was the last time you had a meaningful, personal experience with Jesus?
2. How important is it to you to get "face time" with the Savior? What are you doing to seek His face?
3. When have you asked for God's grace in the form of a blessing?
4. How can you begin to look for God's power in your life, rather than just His provision? What would that look like?

## CHAPTER 6

# THE LOVE THAT CASTS OUT ALL FEAR

FROM THE BEGINNING OF TIME God planned to mightily strengthen you in these last hours. Before you were even conceived, He knew that He would be giving you a miraculous breakthrough over fear through a new dimension of relationship with His Son.

This is a relationship that is founded and rooted in the power of love, a love so powerful that it has overcome the entire world and every unclean spirit in it! God tells us, *"There is no fear in love; but perfect love casteth out fear: because fear hath torment..."* (1 John 4:18). This is a dynamic passage of truth. Before we go any further, let us look at the Amplified Bible's translation of this verse in its entirety. It says:

> *There is no fear in love [dread does not exist], but full-grown (complete, perfect) love turns fear out of doors and expels every trace of terror! For fear brings with it the thought of punishment, and [so] he who is afraid has not reached the full maturity of love [is not yet grown into love's complete perfection]* (1 John 4:18 AMP).

Take a moment now to reread this passage. Allow it to penetrate deeply into your spirit. For this takes us right into the heart of the reason why some of us fail.

We have read the phrase, "perfect love casts out fear," so many times that we have assumed it is always Jesus's love for us that is to do all of the work. However, there is another way of looking at this.

Remember that we are in a covenant relationship with our Lord and with each other. It is a covenant of love, and love is a two-way street. Therefore, not only is it Christ's powerful love for us that casts out fear, but our love for Him should cause us to stand up in union with Him and literally kick that spirit of fear right out the door!

Think about it. When you truly love someone, and become one with them, you love what they love, and hate what they hate. Our relationship with the Lord is no different. Through His Word we are told, *"Ye that love the Lord, hate evil..."* (Psalms 97:10). There is no worse evil than fear.

This being the case, all of you who truly love Him will fervently desire to no longer tolerate all of those fears that are so offensive to Him. You will no longer put up with those vile, fearful thoughts which so brutally block your communion with Him. From now on, you will rise up and refuse to let any fear pollute your heart and mind.

As soon as you take this stand, something dramatic will begin to happen. You will come into an even deeper revelation of His love for you! The cry of your heart will change. Instead of it being a constant plea for deliverance, it will be, *"...that I may know Him [that I may progressively become more deeply and intimately acquainted with Him]..."* (Philippians 3:10 AMP).

And know Him you will. You will come to know Him in a deeper way each time you choose to let your love for Him rise up and, with Him, expel those fears right out of your mind. He will then rush in to fill all of those areas where fear once dwelt, and you are one step closer to being totally restored.

## Grow in Love for Him

By now you may be saying, "What can I do? I don't have that kind of love for the Lord yet. I want to, but I'm not quite there."

Let me help you. Know that He is right there with you, knocking at the door of your heart, longing to come in (see Revelation 3:20). The only problem is that you don't know how to come into the experience of His Presence. You don't know how to open the door. To help you discover where the blockage may be, sit down and ask the Holy Spirit to lead you through the following questions:

- Do I really crave and desire His Presence more than anything else in the world, no matter where I am or what the circumstances are?
- Do I take the time each day to meet with Him, to spend time with Him, time when I'm not begging for anything or dictating to Him but just being still before Him in adoration and worship?
- Do I raise my voice to Him, singing to Him in my heart, praising and thanking Him continually, or do I withhold it because I'm afraid?
- When He asks me to do something, what is my response, and how quick is it?
- Am I totally willing to relinquish my fears (which I have become so accustomed to), so that I might dwell quietly in His peace?
- Do I get so caught up in the cares and works of this world that I postpone devoting myself to a relationship with Him?
- Does He mean more to me than my reputation, the opinions of others, my family, my possessions, or my ambitions, even my ambitions for Him?

- How much does obedience to Him mean to me? Have I completely given Him my will? What price am I willing to pay?
- Do I have any unpaid vows?

Whatever that price is, please do not be afraid. Make up your mind now that you are willing to pay it.

## Discussion Questions

1. What are you currently doing to seek the Lord and grow spiritually?
2. What more can you do to chase after the Lover of your soul?
3. If you can't think of any practical steps, pray and ask God what He thinks you could do to seek Him. Then do it!

CHAPTER 7

# WINNING THE WAR VERSUS WINNING THE BATTLE

BY NOW YOU KNOW HOW vitally important it is for you to begin today to break through and press on to victory. In fact, as soon as you read this book, you might run right out and win your very first battle against fear. "Hallelujah!" you'll shout. "It works!"

But don't be deceived. Winning one battle does not mean you've won the war. Until you win your personal battles against fear and any other demon spirits, you're in no shape to get into the real war for other souls.

Wars are made up of many battles. After your first battle is won, you can expect Satan to try to reclaim lost territory by attacking you in three vital areas—your mind, your emotions, and your will.

Remember that Satan is the father of lies. Soon after the victory, he will try to tell you that you were never delivered in the first place. He will try to deceive you by counterfeiting your past symptoms of fear. He will most certainly try to tempt you with the easy way out the next time fear comes along. What do you do? The apostle James instructs us, *"Submit yourselves therefore to God. Resist the devil, and he will flee from you"* (James 4:7).

Now most of us are pretty good at the submission part, and you can submit all you want. But until you fully determine to also resist Satan, there is no fight. When there is no fight, he automatically wins.

However, the moment you choose to stand and resist, you establish a turning point in the war. No longer are you merely Satan's pawn to push around. You are someone to contend with. As soon as you prove to the devil that you mean business, the battle is on.

> *Therefore put on God's complete armor, that you may be able to resist and stand your ground on the evil day [of danger], and, having done all [the crisis demands], to stand [firmly in your place]. Stand therefore [hold your ground]...* (Ephesians 6:13-14 AMP).

Study the entire sixth chapter of the epistle to the Ephesians for yourself. It holds many keys to spiritual warfare, including the armor you must put on for any offensive encounter with the enemy. Any time you stand facing him, holding firm, and exposing the spirit of fear by calling him by name, you are on the offensive!

Of course, you know by now that this kind of warfare is never easy. Jesus battled so hard in the Garden of Gethsemane that He literally sweat blood. If it wasn't easy for Jesus, it won't be easy for you. But the price of not fighting is perpetual immaturity and spiritual stagnation. The writer of Hebrews warned of this when he admonished believers who were falling behind:

> *You have not yet struggled and fought agonizingly against sin, nor have you resisted and withstood to the point of pouring out your [own] blood* (Hebrews 12:4 AMP).

After 60 years of victorious spiritual warfare, I can tell you that it is at the point when you literally feel (in the spirit) that your own blood is about to be poured out, that God's power sweeps into your being like a flood and the enemy is gone! Is spiritual warfare pretty? No. Will your war against fear be pretty? No. Do you want to grow and be useful to God? Yes! Since you do, God has equipped you with all that you need to do it.

> *(For the weapons of our warfare are not carnal, but mighty through God to the pulling down of strong holds;) Casting down imaginations, and every high thing that exalteth itself against the knowledge of God, and bringing into captivity every thought to the obedience of Christ* (2 Corinthians 10:4-5).

Again, casting down every wayward imagination and bringing every fearful thought to the obedience of Christ will be agonizing at first, but you are not alone. It is all a part of qualifying for God's Army! The apostle Peter described a blow-by-blow account of these spiritual battles (and their outcomes) when he said:

> *...That enemy of yours, the devil, roams around like a lion roaring [in fierce hunger], seeking someone to seize upon and devour. Withstand him; be firm in faith [against his onset—rooted, established, strong, immovable and determined], knowing that the same (identical) sufferings are appointed to your brotherhood...throughout the world. And after you have suffered a little while, the God of all grace...will Himself complete and make you what you ought to be, establish and ground you securely, and strengthen, and settle you. To Him be the dominion (power, authority, rule) forever and ever. Amen (so be it)* (1 Peter 5:8-11 AMP).

## Get Ready for Split-Second Decisions

The United States has an advance military warning system which warns us if missiles have been fired from an enemy country. If they have, we have only ten minutes to wage a counteroffensive attack against the enemy.

Well, I've got news for you. When that demonic spirit of fear launches one of its "fear missiles" at your mind, you don't have ten minutes to wait. You have one split second in which to decide to counterattack.

This decision takes advance preparation. You must be prepared to instantly choose for the Lord and not against Him. What do I mean? I mean that it is possible to have all of the knowledge of what to do, all the grace of God to do it, all the forces of heaven standing by to help you overcome fear, and still, in that last split second when the enemy roars, you can decide to deny God's power and once again go down to defeat.

The choice is yours. What can you do to get ready to choose Christ in an instant? Have your sword ready!

> *Let the high praises of God be in their throats and a two-edged sword in their hands* (Psalms 149:6 AMP).

Have scriptures that banish fear and praise your Lord ready in your heart and on your tongue. Your sword of the Spirit is the Word of God, fueled by your love for Him. When the enemy looms on the horizon, use your weapons! Speak them. Bind the enemy and defeat him with the Word. Let Christ arise within you. Let His enemies be scattered! You are the victorious one!

Decide right now to put on a new mental attitude toward the battles ahead. Put on a spirit of fierce determination and make up your mind that you will choose to press through every time.

The apostle Paul expressed this same valiant determination when he said:

> *Not as though I had already attained, either were already perfect: but I follow after, if that I may apprehend that for which also I am apprehended of Christ Jesus. Brethren, I count not myself to have apprehended: but this one thing I do, forgetting those things which are behind, and reaching forth unto those things which are before, I press toward the mark for the prize of the high calling of God in Christ Jesus* (Philippians 3:12-14).

Then Paul went on to say, *"Let us therefore, as many as be perfect, be thus minded: and if in any thing ye be otherwise minded, God shall reveal even this unto you"* (Philippians 3:15).

Beloved, one day each one of us, like the servants in the Gospel of Matthew, will stand before our Master and account for every talent He has given to us. But also appearing before the throne of God will be countless souls of our generation, crying out to the Father, *"The harvest is past, the summer is ended, and we are not saved"* (Jeremiah 8:20).

Each year over 120 million people are added to the world's population—unreached and unsaved. How can any one of us, knowing what and whom we have been given, stand by and let any demonic spirit of fear hold us back while millions face eternal death?

The summer is almost over. The end-time harvest is nearly finished. Countless souls still have not heard the Gospel, and we will be accountable for each one of them. Can you hear God's battle cry in your heart? He is calling to you now, saying:

> *Have not I commanded you? Be strong, vigorous, and very courageous. Be not afraid, neither be dismayed, for the Lord your God is with you wherever you go* (Joshua 1:9 AMP).

*Wherever you go, break through, and press on in the mighty Name of Jesus!* You are free from fear!

## Discussion Questions

1. What types of thoughts do you have that begin to plant fear in your mind?
2. How do you typically respond to these thoughts?
3. Choose a verse of scripture—use one from this chapter if you like—and write it out and put it somewhere you will see it. Remind yourself of this verse the moment you have a fearful thought.
4. What are you battling spiritually right now? How are you going to prepare for the next attack once you have your victory?

CHAPTER 8

# THE REVELATION OF THE NEW ANOINTING

GOD'S WORD SAYS, *"YE SHALL know the truth, and the truth shall make you free"* (John 8:32). One of the greatest truths that God has ever revealed to me—for fighting and for winning every time, in the great spiritual warfare in which we are engaged—is the revelation of the New Anointing. This revelation not only has revolutionized my life and ministry, but it has done so to the lives and ministries of countless ministers and Christian lay people around the world with whom I have shared this teaching.

I have testimony after testimony on file of people (literally thousands) who have learned these truths and have applied them in their own lives to witness the most amazing answers to prayers that they have ever known. Using these truths, they have prayed in the Spirit to grasp victories that have eluded them for years.

## RETURN TO NORTH AMERICA

It was on the Island of Grenada in the West Indies, in 1964, when God began to reveal the truth of the New Anointing to my heart. At that time, He was using me in a tremendous manner on the foreign fields of this world. Tens of thousands would journey for miles by every conceivable method, often on foot, to attend our crusades in Asia, South and Central America, Korea, and Africa. Multiplied thousands would surrender their lives at the close of every service to accept Jesus as their Savior. Thousands more would be healed of terrible afflictions—goiters, tumors, deafness, lameness, blindness, and arthritis. It was a common sight to see six deaf-mutes healed in one service. God had given me the key to reaching the heathen nations of this world for Jesus Christ.

When ministering, it has always been my custom to lock myself away, alone with God in prayer—no calls, no visits, no sightseeing—every afternoon. As I sought God for the great victories in the Grenada meeting, God spoke to me and said, *"Son, I want you to return to North America."*

Most of my ministry had been spent in the Third World countries, where I had seen the tremendous need of the masses. This new commission to return to North America became one of the biggest hurdles this ministry has ever had to overcome. Although I loved the people of North America, it seemed to me that the need on the foreign field was so much greater.

Although North America only had 6 percent of the world's population, the nation claimed 94 percent of the ministries. That left other nations with 94 percent of the world's teeming billions, and only 6 percent of Christian ministries, including Catholic and Protestant.

God had been blessing our ministry overseas with far greater results than any other ministry in the history of the Church. We had been preaching to tens and even hundreds of thousands of people night after night, up to 250,000 in a single service. As many as 50,000 people would pray the sinner's prayer and surrender their hearts to Christ in a single service.

Why should I leave such a ministry to come back to North America where there are churches on nearly every corner? Most ministers were describing North America as "burned over" with the Gospel. Many thought the time of revival for North America was past.

When God told me to get ready to go back to North America, I was shocked. I tried to bargain with God. I said to Him, "God, give me at least one reason why I should go back to North America."

Then God spoke again and told me, *"Son, judgment is coming to North America."*

That was only part of His message to me. As God continued to speak, He put into my hands and heart one of the greatest positive statements for meeting the crisis that you could possibly imagine. He said, *"I am going to send a new anointing of my divine healing power to North America."*

What a thrill came over my being with that statement! I went into the next service in Grenada knowing beyond the shadow of a doubt that God had spoken. I also knew that there was more His Spirit would reveal to me. There was still a missing link, a key in God's timing.

I kept the revelations and directions God gave me in Grenada hidden in my heart as I continued to be led by Him on a daily basis. I always watched for the key I knew God would give me for using the New Anointing as I continued ministering in the nations of the world.

For years missionary evangelism in foreign lands was done under the assumption that those lands were different from the countries of North America. That assumption was made because clothing, food, shelter, language, and customs were different. In my own ministry, for many, many years, I would use one method in the "civilized" cities of North America, while I used an entirely different method in the overseas countries of South America, Africa and Asia. As God brought a deep spiritual understanding and revelation of what was really happening behind the scenes in every country, my ministry was revolutionized drastically.

## Don't Send Me There

For many years, God sent me to many of the nations of the world; but there was one place on my heart that I prayed, "God, don't You ever send me to this country."

That was before 1970. I had been through this country many times. My plane would stop at the airport and sometimes I could not get a plane out for a day, or sometimes two.

I have been traveling for many years, since long before we had daily flights. Sometimes, we would be in a country and we would not even know if a plane was going out for two or three days. We had to keep going back to the airport every day to find out if our plane was going to be leaving.

I would be stuck in this particular country, sometimes for days when I could not get a plane out. I would go to a restaurant and eat. I would have my food at my table and I could not eat it. I would look around and in the waiter's eyes I could sense the demon powers. I could see it in their spirit. I lost my appetite. I don't think in all of my life, in all my years of passing through this particular country, that I have ever eaten a decent meal that I have enjoyed.

I said, "Lord, don't You ever send me here again."

One day the inevitable happened and God said to me, "Morris, you have had invitations for years to this country. I want you to go." So I accepted an invitation around 1970 and I went to that country for my first crusade there. That country was India!

When I arrived in India in 1970 for the Madras crusade, I was met at the plane by my son, David, who was then just out of high school and was traveling with my advance team.

David's face looked absolutely drained. He was so white he appeared to be ill. "David, what is wrong?" I asked.

He said, "Dad, I don't know! There is something in the air; something about this place is making me sick. I do not understand it."

I knew what it was immediately. Was it the food or water? No. It was spiritual.

I had been to India many times before and I knew of the countless false gods that are worshiped in that country. It was estimated at the time that 650 million people of India served more than 330 million gods. The oppression of demon spirits in the air is so thick that you can feel it. It was this oppression that was making David sick.

Later in my hotel room as I travailed in prayer and fasting for the crusade, there came over me a feeling and a pressure such as I had never known. I felt as though I was literally being torn apart in my innermost being.

I cannot describe the warfare I experienced there in that room as, alone with God, I began to call out various evils by name and bind them in the Name of Jesus. I planted myself in prayer. I began to bind the spirits of sin, the spirits of sickness, the spirits of religion, the spirits of false cults, and the spirit of idol worship.

Something happened to me during that experience in my room. I had known what it was before to pray, but I began to travail in prayer in such a way that I had never experienced before. The only way I could describe it was as if my spirit went out of my body and went into another world. That is why I can understand some of the unutterable groanings that come forth from people.

> *Likewise the Spirit also helpeth our infirmities: for we know not what we should pray for as we ought: but the Spirit itself maketh intercession for us with groanings which cannot be uttered* (Romans 8:26).

I have experienced that. I found, instead of dealing with the things on the surface, such as fanatical Hindu priests, I was dealing with the root cause in the spirit world.

The word went all over that the Hindu priests were going to kill me. Instead of dealing with the fanatical Hindu priests in prayer, I found myself going beyond the surface of things. If those Hindu priests were going to come and create a riot by trying to kill and destroy the crusade, I knew I must go beyond the surface and get hold of the cause.

In this case, what would cause the Hindu priests to riot? Were they rioting on their own? Were they coming against me on their own? Was it just because they were religious, and had a different religion, that they did not like me? Was there a force or was there a controlling spirit making those Hindu priests do something out of control?

I went on like this for almost two days in my room, interceding, travailing, groaning, moaning, battling, and taking hold with power and authority. Something was happening in the spirit world, not on the surface, but in the spirit world. Hour after hour, this binding of evil spirits continued. Finally, victory came. I felt great release, great victory in my spirit.

When I walked out on that platform the first night, there were, conservatively speaking, 70,000 people, many of whom were Hindu priests.

Other missionary evangelists had been to India, but to the best of our knowledge there had never been a successful, completed, full open-air Christian meeting in that country. Billy Graham had a successful meeting there, but we were told it had been held in the compound grounds owned by the Church of India.

There had been several previous attempts, but many platforms were torn down or destroyed. Hindu priests rose up. There were mobs, and several of my evangelist friends barely escaped with their lives. If they had not been protected through the crowd, rushed into cars and taken right to the airport and flown out, they would have been killed. Those Hindu priests were fanatical! They believed if they killed a Christian, they had done one of their 330 million gods a service.

I went up there that night and ministered. You could have heard a pin drop on the ground, it was so quiet. The Holy Spirit captured every person. We went on like that day after day, until the crowd grew to a point where I could not see the end of the people as they fanned out into the black night. We were in what was called the India Athletic Association grounds. It was the size of several football fields, and every inch of the ground was covered wall to wall with people. Picture it—several football fields and beyond.

The only disturbance we ever had during the entire crusade was unclean spirits and demon powers coming out of people as they were thrown to the ground under the power of the Holy Spirit. After they were delivered, we would stand them back up again and they would raise their hands and shout praises to Jesus. We went through our whole campaign in India without one problem. Praise God!

I have gone back again and again to India, and we have seen a marvelous harvest. We have seen the Holy Spirit come on fields of people—not one, but fields with so many people I do not know how you could count them. We have seen 500,000 Hindus in India give their lives to Jesus Christ in one service! This has been because of the Revelation of the New Anointing which God gave to us.

## PRINCIPALITIES AND POWERS

Up until that time, I had been on the foreign field for 17 years. My first overseas crusade was in 1955. Prior to this experience I was well aware of what the Church calls "demon powers." These powers are real!

The anguish I would go through in prayer in order to win victories in these countries was indescribable. I would travail intensely in prayer because I knew I was combating special demonic forces. I was coming to grips with the supernatural powers of the archenemy, Satan. I knew that these powers had to be defeated in prayer before I ever left the prayer room.

Years before, Evan Roberts, the great Welsh revivalist, said these powerful words:

> If missionaries to the heathen recognized the existence of evil spirits, and that the darkness in heathen lands was caused by the prince of the power of the air, and proclaimed to the heathen the message of deliverance from the evil hosts...as well as the remission of sin and victory over sin through the atoning sacrifice of Calvary;

> a vast change would come over the mission field in a few brief years.[1]

This is exactly what we had been doing for years on the great mission fields of the world with the result that thousands upon thousands came to Christ. However, I had never applied this principle in North America, where we think of ourselves as "civilized" people. We are "educated" and "sophisticated." Therefore, I would use an entirely different approach at home than I did on the foreign field.

As I travailed and prevailed in prayer in that hotel room in India, God spoke to my heart in a very unusual way. He said to me, *"Son, you must realize that in the United States of America, in North America, you are not dealing just with ideologies. You are not just dealing with rebellious youth who are disenchanted with the hypocrisy of their parents. You are not just dealing with kids who are trying to tear down the establishment. You are not just dealing with the drug culture or the gay movement. If you will go deep to the root of the problem, you will find that you are in a spiritual battle."*

He revealed to my heart that there were tremendous spirit forces working in North America to tear down the very structure of our society. I believe with all my heart that the devil has assigned special spirits to the task of destroying North America. God showed me explicitly that the key used for such victories on the foreign field, the spiritual binding and defeating of satanic power in the arena of prayer, was the key for victories in North America, just as it had been in the other countries of the world. The warfare was the same.

On the other side of the coin is the great news that we know how to deal victoriously with Satan and we are going to do it. The Bible, God's voice to us, is our real training manual. We can rely upon the Word of God and the Spirit of God to defeat Satan every time, not only in our own lives, but in the lives of our loved ones.

No war is pleasant. No warfare is pretty, spiritual warfare less so than all others. We must stop playing patty-cake with the devil. "Pretty" prayers will never do the job. We must see past our "civilization," our "education," and our "sophistication." We must see the terrors of this warfare and realize what it is we need to combat it. We must learn to press our way through in the Spirit, to the very stronghold of Satan and tear from his grasp the victories of which he has robbed us all these years. We not only must learn it, we must do it!

We must press the battle until every skirmish is over, every victory is ours, until we are more than conquerors in every situation as God has promised we will be: *"In all these things we are more than conquerors through him that loved us"* (Romans 8:37)

We can do it. We will do it as we understand the battle plan and as we move out into the arena of conflict under God's provision and leadership. We must do it, for if something doesn't happen, and soon, the world is on a collision course of spiritual annihilation.

The time has come for God to give you a New Anointing.

## Discussion Questions

1. What are some things that you have to contend with in your life?
2. What are the spiritual forces behind these contentions?
3. Have you seen your enemy as the spiritual force or the person, place, or thing?
4. How can you respond differently, remembering that your battle is with "principalities and powers"—not people?

### Note

1. Jessie Penn-Lewis, *War on the Saints* (New York: Thoms E. Lowe, 1994), 30.

Chapter 9

# AN APPRAISAL OF THE BATTLEFIELD

- Terrorism continues to run rampant on a worldwide basis as confirmed by the daily news broadcasts.
- More babies have been killed in America during the past 35 years than people murdered in all of history's wars!
- An average of 2,260 babies are aborted daily here in the United States.[1]
- Approximately 58,200 children are abducted each year in the United States.[2]
- More than one million young people are sexually molested, filmed, or photographed in the United States for child abusers or for the thriving "kiddie porn" trade.[3]
- In 9 out of 10 cases of child sexual abuse, the abuser is a family member or someone close to the child.[4]
- Since 1980, the number of unwed mothers has jumped 250 percent. Illegitimate births among teenagers jumped from 199,350 in 1970 to 394,370 in 2007.[5]

- One out of every fifteen high school students smoke pot almost daily.[6] The average beginning age of children drinking alcohol is 14 years of age.[7]
- Today nearly half of all marriages end in divorce. About one third of all U.S. families are single-parent families.[8]

These are just a few of the terrible conditions of which we are aware. Every day our newspapers carry similar or worse information. Optimists claim that "things" are going to get better, but are they? And, if so, when?

Listen to what the Word of God says:

> *But evil men and seducers shall wax worse and worse, deceiving, and being deceived* (2 Timothy 3:13).

> *This know also, that in the last days perilous times shall come. For men shall be lovers of their own selves, covetous, boasters, proud, blasphemers, disobedient to parents, unthankful, unholy. Without natural affection, truce-breakers, false accusers, incontinent, fierce, despisers, of those that are good, traitors, heady, high-minded, lovers of pleasures more than lovers of God* (2 Timothy 3:1-4).

It is also a sad fact that under the status quo of the past several years, heathenism has far outstripped the church world.

During the first 200 years after the death, resurrection, and ascension of Jesus, the disciples had reached the whole known world with the influence of Christianity. Almost the whole world was Christian by some definition. Contrast that with the statistics of our day. Although the World Almanac lists 23 percent of the world's population as Christian, their figures include every denomination—Catholic and Protestant—as well as many cults who use the name of Christ, but deny His power and His teachings. It is estimated by many Christian organizations that less than six percent of the world has truly been discipled for Jesus.

With the population continuing to explode in heathen countries, we have reached almost a zero population growth in North America due to birth control, "living together" arrangements, increasing homosexual liaisons, and legalized abortions.

It is estimated that every year over 80 million people are added to the world's population—unsaved, unreached people. When we look at the rise of lawlessness in North America and the mushrooming population of non-Christian and Christian nations, the task before the real Church of Jesus Christ is formidable. Must we withdraw from the arena of life, overwhelmed at what the forces of evil are doing, paralyzed by the weight of population statistics and the desperate needs we see in people's lives?

Not at all. There is an answer. We, as God's children, as His called, chosen, and anointed, are that answer. Jesus said, *"Ye are the light of the world..."* (Matthew 5:14). God's Word also tells us: *"Ye are of God, little children, and have overcome them: because greater is he that is in you, than he that is in the world"* (1 John 4:4). *"In all these things we are more than conquerors through him that loved us"* (Romans 8:37).

God means for us to have victory—total victory! He means for us to take the world for Jesus Christ. It can be done. It must be done. We can do it! However, in order for us to do it, something must happen—it must happen in us!

The Church and the individual Christian have a greater challenge today than at any time in history. In God's dealing with Israel and in the history of the Church, the point of greatest crisis brought forth the greatest manifestations of the power of God.

Man had to seek God for it. It did not come automatically! When Israel began to pray and to seek the face of God, a revelation came that restored the power, that restored the vitality to the spiritual life of the individual and the nation—but man had to seek it. Man must sincerely desire to know and possess this power in order to receive it.

God's answers are not always easy to accept. Sometimes they demand tremendous dedication of our lives. One of the greatest secrets I have learned through times of great trial and decision is to always trust the Holy Spirit. What may at the moment appear difficult may be the very doorway into the most beautiful experience and blessing of your life.

You are approaching such a doorway right now. Do not be afraid to step through it. Victory and power in every area of your life awaits you on the other side.

We have made a spiritual breakthrough which is the revelation of our time. When God gave me the revelation of the New Anointing in Madras, India in 1970, I looked back at the power of the early Church and I began to understand. The early Church, which took almost the entire known world for Christ, had this outlook:

1. They recognized the existence of evil spirits.
2. They knew that evil spirits deceived and possessed men.
3. They understood that the devil was out to hurt, kill, and destroy humankind.
4. They knew that Christ gave His followers authority over them through His name!
5. They recognized their enemy—not things, not surface results.
6. They located their enemy.

The Church of Jesus Christ today, as in the days of its beginning, must lay hold on the spiritual equipment of the apostolic period for dealing with the influx of the evil if it is to take our world for Jesus Christ. This is what the revelation of the New Anointing is all about.

## Discussion Questions

1. How do you feel after reading about the problems of the world today?
2. What are you doing to meet people's needs and share Christ with others?

3. Have you turned a deaf ear and a blind eye to some of these issues? If so, what can you do to confront evil with Christ's love, rather than ignore it or leave it to others to fix?

## NOTES

1. Karen Pazol, et. al., "Abortion Surveillance," Centers for Disease Control and Prevention, November 25, 2011, Results, accessed July 11, 2012, http://www.cdc.gov/mmwr/preview/mmwrhtml/ss6015a1.htm?s_cid=ss6015a1_w.

2. David Finkelhor, Heather Hammer, and Andrea J. Sedlak, "Nonfamily Abducted Children: National Estimates and Characteristics," Missingkids.com, October 2002, Results, accessed July 11, 2012, http://www.missingkids.com/en_US/documents/nismart2_nonfamily.pdf.

3. Roger J.R. Levesque, *Sexual Abuse of Children: A Human Rights Perspective* (Bloomington, IL: Indiana University Press, 1999), 66.

4. National Center for PTSD, "Child Sexual Abuse," U.S. Department of Veterans Affairs, January 1, 2007, Who Commits Sexual Abuse, accessed July 11, 2012, http://www.ptsd.va.gov/public/pages/child-sexual-abuse.asp.

5. Stephanie J. Ventura, "Changing Patterns of Nonmarital Childbearing in the United States," Centers for Disease Control and Prevention, May 2009, Are Births to Unmarried Mothers Mostly to Teenagers?, accessed July 11, 2012, http://www.cdc.gov/nchs/data/databriefs/db18.pdf.

6. Anahad O'Connor, "Marijuana Use Growing Among Teenagers," New York Times Health, December 14, 2011, accessed July 11, 2012,

http://well.blogs.nytimes.com/2011/12/14/marijuana-growing-in-popularity-among-teenagers/.

7. "Alcohol Alert," National Institute on Alcohol Abuse and Alcoholism, January 2006, Underage Drinking, accessed July 11, 2012, http://pubs.niaaa.nih.gov/publications/AA67/AA67.htm.

8. "America's Children: Key National Indicators of Well-Being," Childstats.gov, 2011, Family Structure and Children's Living Arrangements, accessed July 11, 2012, http://www.childstats.gov/americaschildren/famsoc1.asp.

CHAPTER 10

# THE WORLD'S GREAT NEEDS—CAN THEY BE MET?

MATTHEW 9:36 SAYS OF JESUS:

> *But when he saw the multitudes, he was moved with compassion on them, because they fainted, and were scattered abroad, as sheep having no shepherd.*

I have stood before great crowds containing some of the most heartbreaking sights of human need imaginable, and I have met privately with kings, queens, and other very high-ranking leaders. Yet I can truthfully say I have never met a person who did not have some kind of need. You have never met a person who does not have needs, whether or not you are aware of them.

It is not enough, however, just to realize that people have needs. Neither is it enough to be moved with compassion for them. We must provide the answer and the help if we are to work the works of God in our generation. Is there an answer for them? What can you tell them? Where can they find real help?

God has greatly blessed the World Evangelism ministry. One of the greatest things I have to offer is the strength of my prayers, not only in meetings, but alone with God in the power of intercession.

Every month thousands of letters arrive at my office. Many of them contain glowing descriptions of God's blessing and graces, but many of them reflect the bitterness, heartache and poverty of a world under attack. Much of my time is spent in intercessory prayer for the desperate requests.

I cannot share with you the names of the people, for they are confidential, but I do want to share some of the requests that pour into my office daily. It is truly heart-rending. As I share them with you, perhaps some might say, "Why, I could have written that letter myself. That is the same problem I have." Or perhaps you know others who are entangled in the same situation as the writers of these letters.

The mother of a teenage daughter writes:

> Reverend Cerullo, we are members of a traditional church, and have always taken our children to Sunday school. Our daughter was a good girl and was always active in the various church activities, until about a year ago when her attitude started to change. She became very disrespectful of both her father and me, and was very evasive when we would ask her where she was going at night.
>
> I found out last night that she has obtained birth control pills from a public health agency. I know now that she is using drugs with increasing frequency. Both her father and I have tried to reason with her. I have prayed for her, but she only seems to be getting further and further away from us. I fear at any moment she will leave home and we will never see her again. What can I do?

A young wife sent in this heart cry for help:

> Brother Cerullo, I met my husband in church; we were both Spirit-filled believers and very active in church work. This continued after we were married, and through the birth of our two wonderful children. We were happy and

> very much in love; but about six months ago, something strange came over him and he just wasn't the same man that I married. He came home last night and said that he is in love with someone else and wants a divorce. I cried all night long; it seems my world has come to an end. Is there any answer?

A man under bondage to the tobacco habit writes:

> Reverend Cerullo, I have been a Christian for three years. It has been the most glorious period of my life. I have seen many wonderful prayer victories, but I am bound by the cigarette habit and I have done everything I know, but I cannot get free. When I go to buy cigarettes, I feel so embarrassed and so bad that I actually cry, but I cannot help myself. Can you help me?

Lack of thought control, such as that revealed in this letter, is probably the most common cause of a defeated Christian life:

> Brother Cerullo, I am really ashamed to reveal what I am about to write; and unless you can give me some answers, I feel that my Christian life is in jeopardy. I have a wonderful wife and three lovely children. I attend church regularly and even teach Sunday school, but no one, not even my family, knows the turmoil inside me. I cannot get control of my thought life. The most evil imaginations come into my mind. I fight them, but feel powerless to cast them out. I will wake up in the middle of the night with visions of the most immoral things. I have done everything I know. I have prayed, and fasted, but it is only getting worse. What can I do?

Even ministers are not immune from Satan's attacks. There are more pastors leaving the ministry than ever before. Here is a typical reason:

> Brother Cerullo, I have been a successful pastor for the past 15 years, and at the moment we have a lovely church

> and everything on the outside appears to be just beautiful. On the inside it is a different story. I am at the end of my rope. I don't see anything happening in the spiritual lives of my people. I preach about dedication and holiness and most of our congregation has been baptized in the Holy Spirit. The trouble is that I cannot find any fruit of the Spirit. For a midweek dinner we can have a crowd, but for a prayer meeting there is only a handful. Brother Cerullo, I am tired of "playing church" and unless something happens, I am going to seek a secular position. Money is not my motive, but I cannot take the frustration any longer of preaching my heart out and seeing nothing happen. What would you advise me to do?

Another writes of an uncontrollable spirit:

> Reverend Cerullo, I don't know if you can help me, but there is something that is keeping me from the victory that Christ has for my life. I have an uncontrollable temper. What I can't understand is that I will absolutely blow up over the silliest things and afterward I can't really believe that I could allow such little things to bother me. Just when I seem to be gaining ground in my Christian life, some little irritant will cause me to say the most cutting, destructive things to those I love. Each time it seems to be getting worse and it is to the point now that I am actually afraid that I will do some violent thing that even time will not repair. I am desperate.

Sometimes the need is mental anguish, as in these two cases:

> Please pray for my unsaved sister. Evil spirits have taken over her mind and tell her that people are coming into her apartment and poisoning her food. She becomes very ill and cannot eat for many days. She will not accept Jesus in this satanic condition and the devil is turning her against me.

> I had an incurable mental illness. I was labeled paranoid, schizophrenic, manic depressive, suicidal, homicidal....

The incidence of marital violence is shocking:

> I hope this will be the last time my husband will beat me up. Nothing I have done deserves this beating.

Sometimes suicide seems the answer:

> My husband and I had family arguments about his drinking that would lead to a fight and I would always get hurt. I tried to commit suicide and didn't care about cleaning house or being a wife to my husband. Now our four girls are taken away from us until we can become a family.

Concern about loved ones is heart-rending.

> Please pray for my unsaved brother in this newspaper clipping that tells about the arrest of two men who allegedly went on a robbery crime spree. Their car crashed into a chain-link fence. My brother tried to jump into a passing car. He was shot in the shoulder and is in the hospital jail ward.

> Satan is trying to destroy my daughter. She has left her husband and has taken their two small children. She is mixed up in a lot of bad things. Her husband is frightened for the little children.

Personal safety is threatened:

> I am so shocked I can hardly restrain myself. My dear husband of 45 years was kidnapped by two men and forced to drive them around. They took him to the credit union, forced his signature, took all his life savings and mine and left us with only $10.08.

Many feel they have no reason for living at all:

> I don't want to be lonely and lost and insecure and full of fears. I am so disoriented and lost without God's love and compassion. Sometimes I feel that nothing good is happening in my life. It is just a total wreck. I don't have anything to live for.

These letters are all very real. They represent just a few of the thousands that I receive every month from people with every conceivable kind of problem.

The letters show many negatives—trials, defeats, depressions, and frustrations that come into people's lives, even God's people. Why? Just within a very short period of time, a sample of the mail revealed tremendous pressures on God's people:

> My husband is staying with a woman who is using witchcraft. We have five children who have lost all respect for their father.

> I am "gay" and probably the loneliest person in town. I don't know what it is to feel honest love...all I know is lust.

> Satan destroyed my home four years ago. My former wife is in deep sin. My daughter is living with a man. My son is disillusioned and rebellious.

> A neighbor boy is afflicted with a rare bone disease. He can break a bone merely by coughing or sneezing. He is 17 and confined to a wheelchair for the rest of his life unless our Father intervenes.

> My marriage is about over and I can't accept it. I am not saved, nor is my husband. I believe he will die and go to hell, just like me and my children.

> My beloved wife is possessed by devils and lies untreated in a hospital while our retirement resources are being destroyed.

> I lost my baby at birth and my heart is broken. We don't understand why.
>
> I believe it is too late for my salvation. I have a sin on my heart which I don't believe the Precious Lord will forgive me.
>
> My daughter has had a sex change operation and is now a man. It has just about broken my heart.
>
> Our grandsons have been on dope and alcohol. One has almost ruined his mind and has beaten up and injured his father twice.

Others tell of fathers abusing their little girls (and boys) and unspeakable degradation of all sorts that I cannot even share in these pages. There are many, many more in the world out there where you live, work, or minister.

## Answering the Need

To provide those answers is precisely the reason for the preparation of this book. It puts into your hands a manual on spiritual warfare. It reveals the basic force, power, and cause behind all human suffering and tells what you, as a child of God, a member of God's Army, can do about it. Victory is yours!

This study is based on the revelation of the New Anointing which God began to pour into my soul in 1964. I first shared it in a 44-page booklet published in 1972 and then in an enlarged 150-page book entitled *The New Anointing* in 1975. The message has continued to grow and develop, resulting in a comprehensive textbook prepared especially as a teaching tool for our Schools of Ministry.

Ministers and laymen alike who have been touched through the previous books have found their lives completely revolutionized. Thousands of letters in our files testify to how God used these truths to change lives and ministries. Here are excerpts from a few of the letters.

A chaplain from Arcadia, California wrote:

> I have to make a decision for ministry that will probably be the greatest challenge to my life as a minister and Christian. I have been praying for divine guidance and I feel that God has spoken to me through your book.

A pastor from Midland, Georgia wrote:

> Coming back to the church I pastor, there was such a great anointing the people wondered what had happened to me.

A Methodist minister from Illinois wrote:

> I praise God that I received a copy of your book, *The New Anointing*. It was sent from God. Revival has broken out in our church and what this book describes is happening here. Pray for me...I want all that God wants to give.

After reading *The New Anointing*, a minister from South Carolina wrote:

> In my ministry, I come in contact with a lot of young people who are on drugs and God has been good to us in helping some of them find deliverance in Christ. With this new anointing, we could be an even greater blessing to many others.

An Assembly of God minister from Illinois received the teaching and wrote:

> Coming back to my home church, I allowed the Holy Spirit to use me as never before and I began to see outstanding miracles such as I witnessed in Reverend Cerullo's ministry. This power, as Brother Cerullo said, is available for any person who will allow the Holy Spirit to use him.

An Arizona minister concurred:

> As a pastor, I shall never be the same. I have a new vision and a new anointing that has set my ministry afire for God.

The Pastor of a Christian Center in Ohio reported:

> Every day from Monday the revelation became stronger and stronger until now the church I pastor has become alive to this new dimension and we are so excited.

The letters on file reflect many different denominations—Baptist, Methodist, Presbyterian, Pentecostal, Catholic, and Church of Christ—as the New Anointing teaching cuts across denominational barriers to bring fresh new dimensions to ministries.

I pray that these truths will touch your life with the fire and power of God to meet the desperate needs of those in your area of influence.

> *And the things that thou hast heard of me among many witnesses, the same commit thou to faithful men, who shall be able to teach others also* (2 Timothy 2:2).

## Discussion Questions

1. Can you relate to any of the needs shared in the letters in this chapter?
2. Re-read the testimonies of the New Anointing and visualize the effect this anointing could have on these situations and in your own life.

## Chapter 11

# THE GREATEST WARFARE EVER KNOWN

What is the most horrible war or atrocity that your mind can visualize?

Was it the Civil War when hundreds of thousands of mere teenagers were pressed into service; where they were forced to serve under famine conditions with unspeakable sanitation and scant medical attention, with thousands killed, maimed, or scarred for life?

Was it the great conflict known as World War I where more advanced technology resulted in the ability to kill more people in a shorter period of time and again left thousands dead or mutilated?

Was it World War II that not only left the dead, dying, and maimed scattered on the battlefields of Europe, but saw six million Jews perish in the concentration camps of Hitler? What about the atomic bomb dropped on Hiroshima and Nagasaki with the deadly radiation that wiped out thousands of Japanese and left others with horrible lifetime afflictions?

Perhaps you think of the senseless and bloody political purgings such as Vietnam, Uganda, or other dictatorial countries. Your mind may picture with terror some war yet to come, perhaps a nuclear exchange which will wipe out man completely and devastate the earth as depicted in science fiction literature and films.

Bible scholars may think immediately of the record in the Book of Revelation when blood will flow as high as the horses' bridles, or the 39th chapter of Ezekiel which prophesies of those who will be killed and left to be eaten by ravenous birds and beasts of the field.

All war is terrible beyond description—short ones as well as long and bloody ones—but none mentioned, nor indeed any war which ever has been or ever will be, can equal in scope, violence, or catastrophic results the war which has been going on for thousands of years and has claimed millions upon millions of victims—men and women, boys and girls. A war which has destroyed lives, homes, fortunes, health, minds...which has hurt, killed, tormented, and enslaved...which has spared neither infant nor elderly...which has seen no quarter given, but has been and will continue to be a war to the very end of time.

## THE GREATEST WAR OF ALL TIME

The war of which I am speaking is not a war of swords or guns. It is not a war of armed might or nuclear potential. It is a war that embraces all humankind, that does not spare a single person, small or great. It literally, personally, and vitally involves every soul that is ever born into this world without a single exception. This warfare has existed from the beginning of time and can be documented back to the Garden of Eden. It lies at the base of all wars which have ever been fought, all conflicts, all strife, all disasters, whether involving mighty nations or individuals.

It is the war between the only two opposing forces that there are or ever have been in the existence of the world—God and Satan, good and evil. While this warfare has resulted in very real material damage and physical carnage, its roots are neither in the material, nor the physical realm. It is a spiritual battle. It is a battle which pits men one against another, husband against wife, daughter against mother, brother against brother, sister against sister. But the real warfare is and always has been Satan against God, God against Satan.

Many men through the ages, including theologians of great renown, have denied the existence of a real devil, yet the proof of his existence is everywhere. The results of his work are indisputable. Hiding the reality of his existence is one of the cruelest hoaxes he has ever perpetrated on men.

But not all are deceived. Many great men of God have seen his work and testify to his reality. Billy Graham had this to say: "All of us engaged in Christian work are constantly aware of the fact that we have to do battle with supernatural forces and powers. The devil follows me every day.... He tempts me. He is a very real presence to me."

He also declared: "There is a connection between the devil and the increase of drugs, pornography, sexual license, and the occult in the U.S. We see people who are committing all kinds of violence, mass murders, and we have learned they have been involved with the occult. The very word 'witchcraft' stems from the same Greek word as the word 'drugs.'"[1]

Pope Paul VI of the Roman Catholic Church declared: "The smoke of Satan has entered the temple of God through a fissure in the church. ...Evil is not merely a lack of something, but an effective agent, a living, spiritual being, a terrible reality, mysterious and frightening."[2]

Evan Roberts, the great Welsh revivalist, said: "The devil's great purpose, for which he fights, is to keep the world in ignorance of himself, his ways, and his colleagues; and the Church is taking sides with him when siding with ignorance about him."

The Bible itself clearly teaches that Satan is an entity, a being, a real personage:

> *Put on the whole armour of God, that ye may be able to stand against the wiles of the devil. For we wrestle not against flesh and blood, but against principalities, against powers, against the rulers of the darkness of this world, against spiritual wickedness in high places* (Ephesians 6:11-12).
>
> *The thief* [Satan] *cometh not, but for to steal, and to kill, and to destroy...* (John 10:10).

> *Neither give place to the devil* (Ephesians 4:27).
>
> *And that they may recover themselves out of the snare of the devil, who are taken captive by him at his will* (2 Timothy 2:26).
>
> *And I saw an angel come down from heaven, having the key of the bottomless pit and a great chain in his hand. And he laid hold on the dragon, that old serpent, which is the Devil, and Satan, and bound him a thousand years* (Revelation 20:1-2).

Even men who are not known for their religious bent have taken note of the reasons behind the great struggle manifested in the world between nations and ideologies. They see that the real battle of this world is not between countries or ideologies. It is not between people, as noted in Solzhenitsyn's address entitled, "A World Split Apart" delivered at Harvard University several years ago.

Since his expulsion from Russia and his reception of political asylum in the United States was a "cause celebre," one might suppose his address dealt chiefly with the struggle between communism and democracy. His thoughts, however, were much more profound and insightful that that.

"Any of our contemporaries readily identifies two world powers, each of them already capable of entirely destroying the other," he declared. He pointed out, however, that understanding of the split often is limited to a political conception and to the illusion that danger could be abolished through successful diplomatic negotiations or a balance of armed might.[3]

The famed novelist defined the split of which he spoke as a fight between the forces of Good and Evil. He declared, "The fight for our planet, physical and spiritual, a fight of cosmic proportions, is not a vague matter of the future; it has already started. The forces of Evil have begun their decisive offensive, you can feel their pressure...."[4]

Winston Churchill, the great English statesman, realized that warfare was more than man's weapons when he wrote in 1951: "Not only do we march and strive shoulder to shoulder at this moment, under the fire of the enemy on the fields of war or in the air, but also in those realms of thought which are consecrated to the rights and the dignity of man."[5]

So warlike a man as Field Marshal Montgomery wrote in 1968: "A nation must stand for something of spiritual and not only material value, and the key to the decline of the spirit is in religion."[6] Spokesmen from every walk of life realize that something is going on behind the scenes of nations that far outweighs what can be seen with the natural eye. They can only conjecture what may lie ahead.

## TWO SIDES

We are geared to think of many different forces at work in the world—the United States and Russia, Israel and the Arab countries, communism and democracy, battles for key governments, conflicts caused by powerful money or oil interests, the cry for "human rights" coming from many factions and groups. The world is a battleground for many conflicts.

The entire picture, however, boils down to the fact that there are only two forces at work in the world. When we realize that, and when we realize what these two forces are—what they stem from, what their thrust is, what is at stake—we will understand that unless something happens, this world is on a collision course that not only will destroy the world, but will plunge countless millions of men and women, boys and girls into the hopeless torture of an eternal hell.

Some years ago, there was a famous science fiction book entitled *When Worlds Collide* in which scientists discovered another planet on a collision course with the Earth. Their solution was to build space ships or "arks" to transport 500 selected people to another planet for the salvation of the race.

The world today very definitely is on a collision course, not with other worlds but within itself, and no man-made ark can offer the solution.

A far from cheerful picture is set forth in this chapter, but it is a necessary picture. Unless we get the true focus of what is really going on behind the scenes, we never will know what we are combating, much less how to combat it.

The scene is set—God against Satan, good against evil, righteousness against sin. The world is on a collision course, and millions of people will be affected from their homes (families) to their jobs, physically, mentally, spiritually. Does this affect you? And what can we, as children of God, do about it?

## Discussion Questions

1. How does the reality of war—of having to fight to survive—affect the way people live on a daily basis?
2. What might we do differently if we as the Church truly grasped the reality of the spiritual warfare going on around us and in us?
3. What can you do today to start "gearing up" for battle in the spiritual realm?

### Notes

1. Quoted in William G. Allan, *Overlords and Olympians* (East Sussex, UK: Society of Metaphysicians, 1986), 32.
2. *Newsweek*, volume 81, 39.
3. Alexander Solzhenitsyn, "A World Split Apart," Columbia.edu, June 8, 1978, A World Split Apart, accessed July 11, 2012, http://www.columbia.edu/cu/augustine/arch/solzhenitsyn/harvard1978.html.
4. Ibid., Not a Model.
5. Winston Churchill, *The Second World War* (Boston, MA: Houghton Mifflin, 1985), 111.
6. *A History of Warfare* (New York, NY: Morrow, 1983), 566.

## Chapter 12

# LOCATING THE ENEMY

All truth is parallel. That means that whatever is happening over here in the natural world is also happening in a similar manner in the spiritual world. The first rule of warfare, whether it is earthly or spiritual, is that you must locate your enemy.

One of the main reasons that the Church has failed to press in and take this world for Jesus Christ is because it has made converts, not disciples. It has begotten sons...but it has not made them soldiers who know how to wage effective warfare. God has called for a trained and motivated army, and we have failed to mobilize for the battle He has called us to.

The purpose of this chapter is that we may be trained, equipped, and mobilized to wage effective warfare with our adversary (Satan) for dominion over this world. It is designed to enable God's people to turn the stance of Christianity from a defensive holding position to an all-out offensive to conquer in God's Name.

### Know the Enemy

One of the very first rules of successful warfare is that we must know our enemy. We must locate him and concentrate our firepower upon him; otherwise our efforts will be dissipated and ineffective.

The world today is in a state of fear. They know there are powerful enemies at work, but they do not know who or what these enemies are, where to look for them, or how to overcome them. Many of our politicians, sociologists, and psychologists have a very pessimistic outlook on the future. One prominent scientist said, "We give the world ten years." Many leaders agree that "things" cannot go on in the same vein in which they are now progressing.

Our nation is afraid. The world is afraid. People possess a fearful "looking after" concerning the things that are to come upon the face of the earth such as Jesus prophesied in Luke 21.

> *Men's hearts failing them for fear, and for looking after those things which are coming on the earth: for the powers of heaven shall be shaken* (Luke 21:26).

People are afraid all of our water systems will be so polluted that we will not have fresh, clear water to drink anymore. There are already many shortages of food throughout the world and predictions of famine are ominous. The bleakest part of the picture on top of all this is that sin is completely rampant. Evil is with us on an unprecedented scale—rising crime rates, increased violence, murders, mayhem, robbery, sex crimes, drug addiction—all are on the upswing.

God told me: "There are spirits loosed that have been assigned the devilish task of tearing down the structure and the society of this nation, and the sooner you realize you are not dealing with men or with political ideologies, the sooner you will have the victory." There are spirits that are loose in the world.

Somebody said to me, "Brother Cerullo, we don't mention that word 'spirits' in our church anymore because my minister says we are not to scare the people."

Let me ask you a question: How can you fight an enemy you have not located? How can you fight an enemy when you close your eyes and pretend that he does not exist?

A man came to me and said, "Aren't you afraid, Brother Cerullo, that if you talk about spirits, people are going to begin to see things in the air?"

I said to him, "If those things are there, we had better see them!"

There are spirits loose in the world, spirits who have been given the diabolical assignment of tearing down the structure, the foundation of this nation and the nations of the world—the Constitution, the Bible, prayer, and everything that is holy. If every minister, lay person, mother, and father had known the truth about spirits being visited upon our world, they would have saved themselves the chaos and the agony they went through with their children.

One of the cardinal rules of success in any field is that you must deal with people and things as they are, not as you wish them to be. In the face of all the problems and perplexities that come upon us, we must never fail to realize that we are not really dealing with men. We are not dealing with political ideologies. We are not dealing with things! I have no ax to grind with communism, because to me, communism is a defeated enemy. That is not the real problem, or the real issue.

Our warfare is not with men. It is not with the social systems of our day. It is not with political ideologies. We are not in a natural battle; we are in a spiritual conflict. The scripture tells us:

> *For we wrestle not against flesh and blood, but against principalities, against powers, against rulers of the darkness of this world, against spiritual wickedness in high places* (Ephesians 6:12).

In addition to fear, there is also great confusion over our nation. Hardly any political leader will stand up and agree with another on any subject, whether it is economics, sociological problems, foreign policy or any other field. There is great perplexity among our leaders.

Confusion is a spirit. There is a spirit of confusion in the religious world as well as in the political. It exists in denominations, as well as in the lives of individual believers. It is a spirit.

Fear is a spirit. There is a spirit of fear pervading the very atmosphere on an unprecedented scale. People are afraid of so many things. Some of the ills they fear are imaginary, but many are very,

very real. People's hearts actually are failing them from fear of circumstances.

Frustration is a spirit. There is total frustration on every hand. I was told by a leading person in the financial world that many presidents of banks in this country are afraid of what is going to come economically. They are trying to sell their holdings to European and foreign interests. I do not say that to scare you, but so that you will know the total, hopeless frustration that exists at the highest levels of our so-called intelligentsia.

Promiscuousness is a spirit. Promiscuousness exists in the very air. The lowering of moral and spiritual standards has reached the point where it no longer is considered immoral to sell the worst kind of literature openly on the streets of this nation and most other nations of the world.

Two boys can walk into a courtroom in this country and demand a marriage license to be married as husband and husband. The "gay liberation" of homosexuality receives mass television and press exposure to propagate this code of conduct on our nation. Many people are now convinced that we must uphold, protect, and even standardize the "rights" of homosexuals.

There are an estimated 4 million homosexuals in North America.[1] It is estimated that fifteen percent of the total population of San Francisco, one of our largest cities, is homosexual.[2] In that city, the public school curriculum includes a course which presents homosexuality as an "alternative lifestyle." It is a spirit of promiscuousness.

These are just a few of the evil spirits loose in the so-called civilized countries of North America which God revealed to me in my hotel room in India.

## VICTORY!

God made known to me that when we realize, as servants of God and as the Church of Jesus Christ, that we are not dealing with men or ideologies, but with the unseen spirit world, we will have the greatest victory this world has ever seen in the Name of Jesus.

We are not in a natural conflict; we are in a spiritual conflict. It cannot be solved by Washington, D.C.; Ottawa, Canada; or 10 Downing Street, Great Britain. It cannot be resolved by religious or political gimmicks, or by any natural means that man can contrive. It can only be men and women who have power with God, and by men and women who can prevail over the unseen forces of this world.

When you really absorb this revelation, you will have solid understanding beneath your feet for the power to march forward, knowing in whom you have believed. Your life will never be the same again. You will know how to deal with the spirits of rebellion, confusion, frustration, turmoil, lust, promiscuousness, sin, dope, unconcern, selfishness, criticism, fear, anxiety, and many thousands of other spirits which have been loosed upon our world.

Because of this, many modern-day Christians are so confused that they no longer know the will of God. They do not know where to go, what to do, or where to turn. They do not know what decisions to make or in which direction to go.

Many denominations—even strong evangelicals—choose to take the easy road out. They choose either to ignore these conditions or to place them in the hands of the psychologists. They explain that the unusual power of the Holy Spirit present in the lives of the early Church ceased, and therefore we no longer are required to deal from a standpoint of a supernatural demonstration of God's power.

The apostle Paul knew nothing of that frustration and confusion when he confessed:

> *And my speech and my preaching was not with enticing words of man's wisdom, but in demonstration of the Spirit and of power: that your faith should not stand in the wisdom of men, but in the power of God* (1 Corinthians 2:4-5).

He also declared:

> *...I know whom I have believed, and am persuaded that he is able to keep that which I have committed unto him against that day* (2 Timothy 1:12).

There was no confusion in his mind when he wrote:

> *Who shall separate us from the love of Christ? shall tribulation, or distress, or persecution, or famine, or nakedness, or peril, or sword? ...Nay, in all these things we are more than conquerors through him that loved us* (Romans 8:35,37).

All truth is parallel. As evil is a spirit, good is also a spirit. As hate is a spirit which has infiltrated and ruled the nations of this world, so love is a spirit. As frustration and confusion are spirits, so is steadfastness. Sickness is a spirit. It is a result of the curse. God never intended for man's eyes to become dim, his ears to become weak, or even for him to lose his hair. God intended for man to live forever. He never intended for man to die. Man was created in the image of God.

There are three things God never intended for man to posses:

1. Sin
2. Sickness
3. Death

The Bible says we are created in the image of God. Through disobedience, the spirit of sin came into the world, and as a result of sin, the spirits of sickness and death.

Salvation is also a spirit. There are many pastors who will testify that they have preached a message that had nothing to do with salvation, but suddenly they would give an altar call and people would receive Christ as Savior. For three, four, or five weeks in a row, people would be saved in the congregation. There seemed to be a spirit of salvation loosed upon the congregation!

There have been times in a church when there would be two or three services in a row with a special anointing for divine healing.

The preacher did not bring it. He did not create it or even especially teach on it. It just seemed to come. That is because healing is a spirit.

## God Is a Spirit

When Jesus asked the Samaritan woman for a drink of water as related in John 4, the woman asked Him a question: "Tell me this, if You are a prophet," she said, "You say that we ought to worship God at the Temple in the city of Jerusalem. We Samaritans say that we should worship God in this mountain. Where do You say I am supposed to worship?"

Jesus had the answer. He declared:

> *The hour cometh, and now is, when the true worshippers shall worship the Father in spirit and in truth: for the Father seeketh such to worship him.* ***God is a Spirit****: and they that worship him must worship him in spirit and in truth* (John 4:23-24, emphasis added).

God is not confined to a stained-glass window, a robed choir, the stone architecture of a cathedral, or to any historic spot. He is not bound to our traditions, forms, or formalities of worship.

God is not limited to time or space. That is why we can pray in North America and God can answer prayer in India or Africa. There is no limit of time or space because God is a Spirit. He is everywhere present at the same time!

Man is also a spirit. Man is created in the image of God: *"God said, Let us make man in our image, after our likeness..."* (Genesis 1:26). This image of God, however, is not in the physical features of man. It is in the spirit. God gave him (man) a free moral will with the ability to rule his spirit.

The image of God is within us. Because man was created in God's spiritual image, God put him here with divine authority to rule the earth. In this respect, people are like angels. God created the angels with the right of choice. Satan, who formerly was one of the highest-ranking angels, exercised this choice to rebel against

God. One third of the angels exercised their choice to follow Satan and were cast out of heaven with him.

Tragically, man used this spiritual image, this right of choice, to make a wrong choice, to disobey God! God had told Adam:

> *But of the tree of the knowledge of good and evil, thou shalt not eat of it: for in the day that thou eatest thereof thou shalt surely die* (Genesis 2:17).

When Adam disobeyed God and sinned, he opened the door for humankind to reap three things that God did not intend for man to possess—sin, sickness, and death. Adam did not die physically on that very day, but he died spiritually. First Corinthians 15:22 says that, "*...in Adam all die.*" It also says that, "*...in Christ shall all be made alive.*" As with Adam, humankind experienced spiritual death, but Christ offers the opportunity to be reborn spiritually.

It is the spiritual part of man that is in God's image. Man is not his physical body. The body returns to dust from whence it came. It is the spirit, God's image, that is the real you, that will live on through eternity. That is why Henry Wadsworth Longfellow could pen these words: "Dust thou art, to dust returnest, was not spoken of the soul."

Man is a spirit. God is a spirit. Satan also is spirit.

> *For we wrestle not against flesh and blood, but against principalities, against powers, against the rulers of the darkness of this world, against spiritual wickedness in high places* (Ephesians 6:12).

To know this truth is to have located our enemy, to have pinpointed the crux of every conflict. We are not in a natural battle in our problems, in our sicknesses, anxieties, fears, and frustrations. We are in a spiritual warfare in the spirit world. This is the root cause of every problem, every battle, every fear, every frustration we have.

Often when I tell people the problems they are having in their lives are the result of the spirits of Satan, their reaction is usually,

"Brother Cerullo, are you going off the deep end and saying that every problem is a demon, or the result of the activities of demons?"

If you walk by a pond and see a fowl with a beak swimming on it, and the sound that fowl makes is "quack, quack, quack," common sense tells you that fowl is a duck. You call it a duck because it looks like a duck, swims like a duck, acts like a duck, and sounds like a duck. When things come upon humankind today that look and act like demon power and fulfill the scriptural description, we do not need to be afraid to call them exactly what they are!

Many people are afraid to identify the world of demon power, because they do not have any idea how to deal with it. They do not know how to go in, press the battle against the enemy, and defeat him in the spirit world! If we can use our psychology and sociology to call insanity, criminality, and perversity an "emotional distress resulting from a maladjusted childhood," or if we can use some other theory to justify the problems which plague our generation, then it can be dealt with in the natural mind. This approach, however, will never find a permanent cure, because the problem is a spiritual problem.

If we define the problem as it really is—the spiritual power of Satan which has gotten into lives through the original entrance of sin—we can deal with it as a sinister spiritual power at the root cause. We can go in with the supernatural power of God, the anointing of the Holy Spirit, and defeat the enemy in the Name of Jesus.

The Church today is at a critical junction in history. The road the Church follows is running into an attack by the devil as never before. The road that crosses ours is the devil's power. Because Satan knows that he has but a short season, the Church is facing a challenge of the devil's power it has never faced before.

However, I know beyond a shadow of a doubt how to meet that challenge. God said: "*...upon this rock* (Jesus) *I will build my church; and the gates of hell shall not prevail against it*" (Matthew 16:18).

We are not just in a holding war, the "hold the fort" kind that some churches sing about, hanging on by the skin of our teeth. Ours is an aggressive war, an offensive strategy. We must take the initiative to invade Satan's own territory, carry the battle to his field, overcome him on every hand, and come out of the battle with the spoils of victory held aloft in the hands of a triumphant Church—in the Name and power of Jesus Christ.

There is something that you possess in your life as a Christian of which the devil is deathly afraid. He is no match for it. It is your ultimate assurance of total victory. As God opens to you the revelation of the New Anointing, you are going to have prayer victories such as you have never before experienced. You will experience victories in your life and see them in the lives of your loved ones as never before.

We know who the enemy is, and God has given us the tools of victory. By His power we will take the battleground for God. Total victory is yours!

## Discussion Questions

1. What are some of the spirits coming against you right now?
2. How can you strengthen your spirit for the fight? Remember whose Spirit is your greatest ally!

### Notes

1. Clay Chiles, "Gay Population In U.S. Estimated At 4 Million, Gary Gates Says," *The Huffington Post*, April 07, 2011, accessed July 11, 2012, http://www.huffingtonpost.com/2011/04/07/gay-population-us-estimate_n_846348.html.
2. "Demographics of Sexual Orientation," Wikipedia, May 07, 2012, Top Cities, accessed July 11, 2012, http://en.wikipedia.org/wiki/Demographics_of_sexual_orientation.

CHAPTER 13

# SATAN'S ORIGIN AND MOTIVATION

AS VIOLENT AS THE WARFARE between good and evil has been, and as long as it has been going on, it is not eternal. God has no beginning of days nor ending. He is from everlasting to everlasting. That is not true of Satan. God is eternal. Satan is not. God is the great I AM—ever existent. Not only was He in the beginning, He was before the beginning. He made the beginning. He is the beginning, and He will continue to exist eternally without end!

Satan did have a beginning, and there will come a time when he will meet his just end. His beginning was as a heavenly being created by God—not as the bearded caricature we often see pictured by artists, but as a glorious creature of magnificence in the heavenlies. His name at that time was Lucifer, which literally means "light-bearer." Isaiah refers to him as Lucifer, son of the morning (see Isaiah 14:12).

Ezekiel carries this description of Lucifer's former glory:

> *...Thus saith the Lord God; Thou sealest up the sum, full of wisdom, and perfect in beauty. Thou has been in Eden, the garden of God; every precious stone was thy covering, the sardius, topaz, and the diamond, the beryl, the onyx, and the jasper, the sapphire, the emerald, and the carbuncle, and*

> *gold: the workmanship of thy tabrets and of thy pipes was prepared in thee in the day that thou was created. Thou art the anointed cherub that covereth; and I have set thee so: thou wast upon the holy mountain of God; thou hast walked up and down in the midst of the stones of fire. Thou wast perfect in thy ways from the day that thou wast created, till iniquity was found in thee* (Ezekiel 28:12-15).

Because of Lucifer's pride, self-exaltation, and rebellion, he came under God's judgment and was cast out of heaven. These events also were described by Ezekiel:

> *By the multitude of thy merchandise they have filled the midst of thee with violence, and thou hast sinned: therefore I will cast thee as profane out of the mountain of God: and I will destroy thee, O covering cherub, from the midst of the stones of fire. Thine heart was lifted up because of thy beauty, thou hast corrupted thy wisdom by reason of thy brightness...* (Ezekiel 28:16-17).

The event was also recorded by Isaiah who gave further details of Lucifer's transgression:

> *How art thou fallen from heaven, O Lucifer, son of the morning! how art thou cut down to the ground, which didst weaken the nations! For thou hast said in thine heart, I will ascend into heaven, I will exalt my throne above the stars of God: I will sit also upon the mount of the congregation, in the sides of the north: I will ascend above the heights of the clouds; I will be like the most High* (Isaiah 14:12-14).

Impressed with his own beauty and high rank as the "cherub that covereth," Lucifer became obsessed with the desire to usurp God's throne, take over heaven, and himself become the object of worship. He was severely judged by God for this rebellion with the assurance of far greater punishment to come. However, Lucifer never lost his burning desire to be worshiped. From that desire and Satan's hatred of God stems all the havoc which has taken its ugly toll in the lives of people down through the ages.

Lucifer (now known as "Satan," the "devil," "adversary," etc.), in seeking to achieve dominion in heaven, led a rebellion among the angels, recruiting vast numbers of them for his own purposes. This rebellion was put down by God and Satan was cast out of heaven.

## NOTHING COULD BE FURTHER FROM THE TRUTH.

Everyone has seen the caricatures which depict Satan with pointed ears and tail, dressed in a red suit, with a wicked gleam in his eye and a pitchfork in his hand.

> *For we wrestle not against flesh and blood, but against principalities, against powers, against the rulers of the darkness of this world, against spiritual wickedness in high places* (Ephesians 6:12).

We confront not only Satan, but hordes of principalities and powers. Evil spirits come against us to seek our destruction by causing us to disobey God and His commandments and walk in the flesh, thereby robbing the Spirit.

## GOD GAVE MAN DOMINION

Many people wrongfully suppose that when God cast Lucifer out of heaven, he gave Satan the world for his domain. That is not so, for we read in Genesis that God gave dominion of this earth to man, who was His crowning creation. In the six days of creation described in Genesis 1 and 2, God brought forth a perfect creation on this earth through His creative Word.

On the first day, He said, "Let there be light" and there was light. On the second day, He made the firmaments of the heavens. On the third day, God said:

> *Let the waters under the heaven be gathered together unto one place, and let the dry land appear: and it was so* (Genesis 1:9).

When God looked over what His Word had performed to that point, we read: "*...God saw that it was good*" (Genesis 1:10). God continued with further work on that third day, and it was again noted that *"it was good"* (verse 12).

On the fourth day when God created the luminaries (sun, moon, and stars) and on the fifth day when He created the fowls of the air, fish of the sea, and the beast and cattle of this earth, each time it is noted: *"...God saw that it was good"* (Genesis 1:18,21). Then came the creation of man.

> *And God said, Let us make man in our image, after our likeness.... So God created man in his own image, in the image of God created he him; male and female created he them* (Genesis 1:26-27).

This act took place on the sixth day. When God looked back over what he had done on that particular day, it was not just "good" as other days had been, but we read that *"...behold, it was very good"* (Genesis 1:31). The creation of the sixth day was viewed with a great deal more satisfaction than the preceding five days had been, not just because of the creation of man, but because God announced His great plan for blessing humankind.

> *And God blessed them, and God said unto them, Be fruitful, and multiply, and replenish the earth, and subdue it: and have dominion over the fish of the sea, and over the fowl of the air, and over every living thing that moveth upon the earth. And God said, Behold, I have given you every herb bearing seed, which is upon the face of all the earth, and every tree, in which is the fruit of a tree yielding seed; to you it shall be for meat. And to every beast of the earth, and to every fowl of the air, and to every thing that creepeth upon the earth, wherein there is life, I have given every green herb for meat: and it was so. And God saw every thing that he had made, and behold, it was very good. And the evening and the morning were the sixth day* (Genesis 1:28-31).

Besides man himself, God included something else very important in that day's satisfactory creation. He included his plan for man.

God blessed man. That was part of his plan. He told man to be fruitful, multiply, and replenish the earth. That was part of His plan.

God gave man dominion over everything He had made on earth—over the fish of the sea, the fowl of the air, over every living thing that moved on the earth. He also gave him the bounty of the plentiful food supply brought forth by the vegetation.

God gave man dominion. That was His plan for man. This dominion is a very integral, very vital part of that day's creation and is the very crux of the study we have undertaken on spiritual warfare.

God gave man dominion. This creation over which God gave man dominion is more fully described in Chapter two of Genesis, which describes the Garden of Eden God planted and gave to man as his natural habitat.

You can see how this chapter repudiates the theory held by many Christians that when God cast Satan out of heaven, He sent Satan down to earth and made him the prince or god of this world. *Nothing could be further from the truth.* God gave man dominion over this world and everything that is in it. He gave into Adam's hands the keys of dominion of this earth.

One has only to read today's headlines, listen to the heartaches of people, or just see the condition of people on the streets to know that this is not the situation as it exists today. *It is easy to see that, instead of having dominion, man is under dominion.* You can see from the open wickedness of the land, from the cruel tragedies which are a daily occurrence, that man is not in control. He is under bondage, in slavery to forces outside himself.

You can see from people's lives and from hearing their heartaches that Satan has taken the dominion away from man and is usurping the great blessings that God intended for man to have. Why? What has happened? Why isn't man using the keys of dominion he was given? *Because he gave them away.* Adam took the keys of dominion that God gave to him and he handed them over to Satan.

## Man Handed the Keys to Satan

Along with the blessings that God gave man in the Garden of Eden, along with the duty of dressing and keeping the garden, along with dominion over every living thing, God gave man one more very important thing. He gave him responsibility.

> *And out of the ground made the Lord God to grow every tree that is pleasant to the sight, and good for food; the tree of life also in the midst of the garden, and the tree of knowledge of good and evil. ...And the Lord God commanded the man, saying, Of every tree of the garden thou mayest freely eat; but of the tree of the knowledge of good and evil, thou shalt not eat of it: for in the day that thou eatest thereof thou shalt surely die* (Genesis 2:9,16-17).

Earlier, we discussed the fact that when God made man in His own image, this was not a physical image, but this likeness of God is in man's spirit. This image included the right of a free will, the right of choice. This right of choice was given to the angels also, for it was Lucifer's choice to exalt his throne as the throne of God.

Man was given a free will, the right of choice, but he also was given the responsibility to exercise that choice in obedience to God's revealed will. The simple test that God set for that obedience was to forbid Adam and Eve to eat of one tree out of all the trees He had provided, the tree of this knowledge of good and evil.

This brings us to the setting for the most cataclysmic event ever to take place on the face of the earth. Adam and Eve, created in innocence and perfection with no sin in their spirits, no sickness in their bodies, were placed in a beautiful garden paradise with all its lovely creations at their fingertips, and they had dominion. Into this idyllic scene came Lucifer, now called Satan, the adversary. Homeless, stripped of the splendor and prestige he once knew, Satan was in a rage at God. He wanted revenge. He wanted to strike back. How could he do it? God is invulnerable. He is invincible. There was no way Satan could strike directly at Him.

As Satan saw the sweet communion between God and man, and the love God had for man, Satan formulated his diabolical plan. Having failed to gain dominion in heaven from God, he would take dominion on earth from man. In so doing, he not only would have the worship and adoration he always wanted, he would get back at God by striking at man, the apple of God's eye, His crowning creation.

> *For thus saith the Lord of hosts...he that toucheth you toucheth the apple of his eye* (Zechariah 2:8).

Satan did not present himself to humankind in the form that has been widely believed for centuries. Nothing could be further from the truth. In the first place, Satan is a spirit, although he can manifest himself in other forms. Secondly, he does not usually advertise his wickedness. Most often he comes in disguise as an angel of light: "*...Satan himself is transformed into an angel of light*" (2 Corinthians 11:14).

To make his entrance into the Garden of Eden for his attack upon God's perfect creation, Satan chose to come in the form of the serpent, not only the most subtle, most cunning of all the creatures, but one of the most beautiful. The serpent at that time was not a snake as we know it today, crawling in the dust; but an upright creation that glittered with beauty. He came in beauty, and he came as an angel of light, to set Adam and Even "straight" about what God had told them:

> *Now the serpent was more subtil than any beast of the field which the Lord God had made. And he said unto the woman, Yea, hath God said, Ye shall not eat of every tree of the garden? And the woman said unto the serpent, We may eat of the fruit of the trees of the garden: but of the fruit of the tree which is in the midst of the garden, God hath said, Ye shall not eat of it, neither shall ye touch it, lest ye die. And the serpent said unto the woman, Ye shall not surely die: for God doth know that in the day ye eat thereof, then your eyes*

> *shall be opened and ye shall be as gods, knowing good and evil* (Genesis 3:1-5).

There have been many cartoons and advertisements which depict a lighthearted Eve biting into an apple. The episode of her disobedience to God has been made to look like a "fun" thing. Even more serious-minded individuals and many ministers of God often fail to see the agonizing destruction to humankind inherent in this one seemingly simple act.

> *And when the woman saw that the tree was good for food, and that it was pleasant to the eyes, and a tree to be desired to make one wise, she took of the fruit thereof, and did eat, and gave also unto her husband with her; and he did eat* (Genesis 3:6).

Let me stress to you the importance of what transpired here. This was more than a man and a woman eating a piece of fruit out of curiosity or to satisfy their appetites. This is one of the most chilling acts that ever took place. Here was a man, Adam, holding the keys of dominion of this world as given to him by God, and in willful disobedience to God's revealed will, in willful obedience to the influence of Satan, he ate of the fruit which God had forbidden him. In doing so, man handed to Satan, God's archenemy, the keys to the dominion of the world. He bowed to Satan. He gave into Satan's hands what God had put in the hands of man.

With this one act of disobedience, Adam abdicated as the ruler of this world and helped Satan onto the throne of dominion. What Satan had failed to accomplish in heaven with the help of rebellious angels, he accomplished in one fell swoop upon earth with the willful cooperation of man. This why Satan is described as "god of this world" in Second Corinthians:

> *In whom the god of this world hath blinded the minds of them which believe not, lest the light of the glorious gospel of Christ, who is the image of God, should shine unto them* (2 Corinthians 4:4).

The coup which gave Satan dominion over fallen humankind opened the door in God's perfect creation for imperfection. It not only marked the entrance of sin into this world, but it paved the way for the entrance of two other great evils God never intended for man to have—sickness and death.

This one act of disobedience on man's part and the transfer of the keys of dominion from man to Satan is what set in motion the great spiritual warfare which exists to this very day and is the basis for all the sin, sorrow, and sickness in the world. Every battle man has ever had, or will ever have, is because of this fact. That is why it is so important for us to know how to deal with it as we face the battles of this life and reclaim the dominion God meant for man to have.

## Discussion Questions

1. Are there some things we tend to assume are just "Satan's domain"—things we can't do anything about?
2. How can we begin to reclaim those lost territories for Christ?

CHAPTER 14

# SATAN'S DOMAIN AND SPHERE OF ACTIVITY

IF GOD DID NOT CAST Satan down to have dominion over this earth, where did He cast him and where is his seat of authority? The book of Job gives a remarkable picture of the wide sphere of activity which Satan enjoys.

> *Now there was a day when the sons of God came to present themselves before the Lord, and Satan came also among them. And the Lord said unto Satan, Whence comest thou? Then Satan answered the Lord, and said, From going to and fro in the earth, and from walking up and down in it* (Job 1:6-7).

It is immediately apparent that Satan has access both to God's Presence and to the whole range of the earth. Though his activities differ in those two places, his aim is always the same—attack!

## THE DEVIL'S STRATEGIES

What he does before God's Presence is to accuse God, to accuse God's Word, and to accuse God's people. "*...which accused them before our God day and night*" (Revelation 12:10). That is what he was doing to Job at the instance quoted above and which we will explore more fully in the following chapter.

Now, what is Satan doing on earth? He is creating the situations that enable him to accuse God by tempting, harassing, tormenting, and attacking man in any way he can. Peter tells us that Satan's travels up and down this world are those of a roaring lion.

> *Be sober, be vigilant; because your adversary the devil, as a roaring lion, walketh about, seeking whom he may devour* (1 Peter 5:8).

Paul tells us he exercises great cunning: "*...Satan himself is transformed into an angel of light*" (2 Corinthians 11:14). The motivation is still the same.

From this picture we get of Satan's widespread evil activities, it would be easy to draw the conclusion that, like God, Satan is omnipresent. This is not so. To know and understand that fact will help us to understand how much greater God is than Satan and how much greater our power against him.

> *Ye are of God, little children, and have overcome them; because greater is he that is in you, than he that is in the world* (1 John 4:4).

We have already seen that Satan is not eternal, and now we see that he is not present everywhere at once. How can we then explain the wide scope of evil which is experienced in all the world at the same time? It is because Satan has a large following of fallen angels or demon spirits to help him carry out his activities.

> *For we wrestle not against flesh and blood, but against principalities, against powers, against rulers of the darkness of this world, against spiritual wickedness in high places* (Ephesians 6:12).

This scripture clearly shows a multiplicity of evil beings—principalities, powers, and rulers. A principality is the state and authority of a prince. Therefore it is apparent that Satan has set up governments and divisions of territory among various rulers. If there are rulers, there must also be those who are ruled, and so it is difficult to even estimate how many evil beings Satan has in his service.

A faint insight is given in the story of the madman of Gadara whom Jesus delivered from demon possession (see Mark 5:1-15; Luke 8:26-35). When Jesus asked the madman his name, he said it was *Legion*, because many devils had entered into him (see Luke 8:30).

"Legion" is a military term. At the time of the Scripture, the term was used by the Roman military to designate a military unit of 3,000 to 6,000 trained and armed men. Use of the term here would indicate not only a large number of demons, but that they were in military ranks of varying authority. We do not know exactly how many demons possessed the man of Gadara, but certainly enough to possess an entire herd of 2,000 swine and cause them to violently destroy themselves (see Mark 5:13).

Despite the number and strength of Satan's legions, however, we need not fear the outcome of the battle.

> *His tail* [the dragon's] *drew the third part of the stars of heaven, and did cast them to the earth...* (Revelation 12:4).

From Revelation 12:4 and ensuing verses, we get the figure that Satan took a third of heaven's angels with him when he rebelled. That means two-thirds remained faithful to God—twice as many as Satan has. There are other great pluses to these figures: God is omnipresent and since He is Creator, He could easily create all the angels needed for any service. Even without angels, God Himself is Almighty, and just His Word is able to meet every need.

## Spirit Beings

Though this study is not the study of good angels, let us mention briefly their use by God. Angels ministered to Jesus after He underwent His temptation at the hands of Satan, *"Then the devil leaveth Him, and, behold, angels came and ministered unto Him"* (Matthew 4:11). Satan knew God's promise to Jesus was that angels would protect Him.

> *...He shall give His angels charge concerning thee: and in their hands they shall bear thee up, lest at any time thou dash thy foot against a stone* (Matthew 4:6).

Likewise, the angels of God minister to us and protect us:

> *The angel of the Lord encampeth round about them that fear Him, and delivereth them* (Psalms 34:7).

> *And of the angels he saith, Who maketh his angels spirits and His ministers a flame of fire* (Hebrews 1:7).

God administers His angels from heaven where His throne is above all.

Satan's hordes are described as the "*rulers of the darkness of this world*" (Ephesians 6:12). This term, as well as the description in the book of Revelation, reveals that his headquarters are in the depths of the earth.

Revelation 9:1 tells of the star that fell from heaven to earth and was given the key of the bottomless pit. From this pit, he will let forth unspeakable creatures during the tribulation period to torment men. Revelation 9:11 says:

> *And they had a king over them, which is the angel of the bottomless pit, whose name in the Hebrew tongue is Abaddon, but in the Greek tongue hath his name Apollyon.*

Also, Revelation 11:7 tells us that the beast as the Antichrist will come out of the bottomless pit.

> *And when they shall have finished their testimony, the beast that ascendeth out of the bottomless pit shall make war against them, and shall overcome them, and kill them* (Revelation 11:7).

It seems certain, therefore, that in the darkness of the earth's depths is where the throne room of Satan is located. Some have held that his throne is in the "heavenlies"—not God's place of abode, heaven, but earth's atmosphere. They use as their authority for this the scripture that speaks of "spiritual wickedness in high places."

Without a doubt, Satan is operating in a lively way in the atmosphere as well as in the "high places" of men's affairs—governmental, religious, financial, etc. However, it is safe to assume that his throne is in the depths of darkness.

As Satan engaged in spiritual warfare against God's heaven and man's domain, there came One who arose and thundered in victory into the very stronghold of Satan's empire to claim the souls of the righteous dead from their place of rest and transport them to the Presence of God. "*...When he ascended up on high, he led captivity captive...*" (Ephesians 4:8). As He did so, He left His footprint on Satan's face as a seal and promise that one day He will bring the wicked one under complete dominion and wipe out his influence forever.

> *And I will put enmity between thee and the woman, and between thy seed and her seed; it shall bruise thy head, and thou shalt bruise his heel* (Genesis 3:15).

> *From henceforth expecting till His enemies be made his footstool* (Hebrews 10:13).

That time has not yet come, however, and so Satan's evil workings continue in the affairs of men and nations today. How he operates even in the lives of righteous people is an area of great misunderstanding which we will address in the following chapter.

## Discussion Question

1. Just how strong is God? If Satan had tricked every last angel in heaven, would God be outnumbered?

## Chapter 15

# SATAN'S CLAIM ON THE RIGHTEOUS

One of the most important questions with which we deal in conducting effective spiritual warfare is this: "Why do the righteous suffer?"[1] This question is not why sinners suffer, why the ungodly suffer, but why—when men and women are living for God with all of their hearts and are doing everything they know to please God—*why* do they suffer from sickness, from accidents, from lost loved ones, from their children getting involved in drugs, from financial failures, from all kinds of tragedies and afflictions?

"Why" is perhaps the most perplexing question that any Christian ever has to face in his entire spiritual life. My mail every week is full of "why" letters. People write for prayer—they want help, and they are seeking answers.

"Reverend Cerullo, I've lived for God all of my life. I've raised my children in the church and taught them about God, but look at them. They have run away from home. They're into drugs. They're in jail. They're alcoholics. Brother Cerullo, why?"

"Revered Cerullo, I'm serving God with all my heart. I pay my tithes, but I keep having unforeseen expenses. I just can't seem to get ahead. I am always in a financial bind. Why?"

"I have been prayed for over many times, Brother Cerullo. I see people all around me getting healed, but I don't get my healing. Why? What is wrong with me?"

"Brother Cerullo, I tried to keep my family in church. We read the Bible and prayed together. But now my wife (or husband) has run off with someone else and left me to raise our little children alone. Why did this happen to me?"

These are just a few of the types of questions that continually pour into my office from the hearts of troubled people. Let me share with you a heart-rending letter received from an elderly lady.

## A Letter of Tears

> Reverend Cerullo,
>
> I believe in the power of prayer. But in 73 years I have suffered so much, to a point where I had not a bed to sleep in or a place to call home. Reverend Cerullo, I'm alone, though I have three children. I have not seen two of them for 20 years. One I see, but his wife holds him around her wrist. I only saw him once a year ago at a funeral, but it was not a mother and son meeting.
>
> I never did drink or smoke or ever do anything to hurt myself or to make the Lord angry at me. But I cannot suffer anymore. I am too old to go on. But your Deeper Life seems to say there is hope. I love the Lord; why do I suffer so? I love my children very much. I would die for them.
>
> My body is broken, tired from trying to work for the roof over my head. I've asked the Lord to help me 100 times a day, a prayer from my inner being. Why do I suffer? Why do my dear children forget me? Thank you for reading my letter of tears.
>
> Yours in Spirit,
>
> Mrs. C.C.

There is no age or generation gap in suffering. This lady from a Florida city is only 21 years old, yet listen to her letter:

> Reverend Cerullo,
>
> My prayer request is I am lonely. Pray that I may find a husband. I have very bad bones in both of my legs. I had four operations to correct them. My muscles are very weak so that I sometimes tremble when I walk. I tried exercise, but nothing happened. I have been mistreated ever since I was 12 years old by my teacher and the children in my school. I also was operated on when I was 12. They made my leg look crooked and everybody picks on me. I guess that is why I am so lonely. I quit school when I was 16 years old because I couldn't stand it any longer.
>
> Now I am 21 years old and nothing has changed. I am lonesome, unhappy, still being picked on and my legs are getting worse. I don't know how much more I can take. I am at the end of my rope.
>
> Reverend Cerullo, I hope I am not taking up too much of your time, but I had to talk to someone and I feel that it should be you. I read your books and I believe in you and pray. I pray a lot, but my prayers don't seem to help. I tried to kill myself once. My mother won't ever listen to me. I can't eat at times. I lose weight and the doctors seem as if they can't help me. I took vitamins but they didn't help.
>
> The only place I go is to church and I sing in the choir. I am not a bad person and don't do evil things. That's why I can't understand why I am suffering so long. I don't do anything. I can't stand it anymore. I would rather die than suffer any longer. Please, please help me. Pray for me, also. I am nervous too; that is why my writing is bad. Oh please, pray and help me.

> Yours in God's Name,
>
> H.G.

A man wrote:

> I am tired of living in poverty. Why can't I get a financial miracle, funds for a home, furniture, a car? Why can't I get a healing for my leg? When? Twenty-five months in a cast, and I can't work. I'm just helpless.
>
> God can help. Did He forsake me? Did He leave me out? Am I not a child of God? Sinners get blessed financially, healing, prosperity. Where do I stand? Doesn't God hear my petition?

My files are full of such desperate pleas. Such questions are everywhere, in the church as well as in the home.

It is easy to understand why the unrighteous suffer, why the alcoholic's home breaks up, why the drug addict gets put in jail, or why the sexually promiscuous ends up in the hospital. They have broken laws, many times both the laws of man and the laws of God. Both earthly and spiritual laws carry penalties if they are broken.

When Saul of Tarsus (who became Paul the apostle) was on the road to Damascus to further persecute the Christians of that day, the Lord overtook him in a dramatic vision and visitation. One of the things Jesus said to him was: *"...it is hard for you to kick against the goads"* (Acts 9:5 NKJV).

Proverbs 13:15 tells us: *"...the way of transgressors is hard."* The Living Bible says: *"the rebel walks a thorny, treacherous road..."* (Proverbs 22:5 TLB). But what about the man or woman who is not kicking against the goads and yet is suffering untold agony of heart and mind? What about the non-transgressor who finds himself helpless on a bed of affliction? What about the non-rebel who finds his pathway full of thorny problems? Is there an answer? If so, what is the answer?

God's relationship with man always has been a relationship of love and complete caring. His intention for man was total health, total provision, total happiness, total prosperity, total well-being in all things—salvation, "to be made a totally whole person." The sin, sickness, death, sorrow, pain, war, and hurt that is in the world today did not come out of God's relationship with man. No unhappiness or sorrow springs from the blessing of God's relationship with man.

Every unhappiness, every sorrow that has ever come upon this world or upon humankind was caused by man's disobedience to God. Man's relationship to God is that man is under the curse of his own disobedience to God. However, sin and disobedience did not bring a change in God's vital relationship to man. That relationship had been one of love, caring, and provision. It is still the same relationship of love today.

If God's relationship to man is one of love, and if our relationship to God is one of obedience and trust, yet trials, tests, pain, suffering and tragedy come into our lives, then we must look behind the scenes for a hidden reason—something we are not able to see with our natural eye.

## Job's Suffering

The biblical account of the multifaceted trials of Job not only gives a dramatic answer to our questions, but furnishes us with a parallel which makes that answer relevant to the ordeals we go through in our own lives. Job is the perfect example of why the righteous suffer. A look at him as our parallel of truth will unlock one of the greatest mysteries of the world to us.

In the first place, Job was no ordinary man. He was a highly honored individual. He had wealth, prosperity, many possessions, and a fine family. The biggest item on the credit ledger of Job's life was that he was a godly man. He feared the Lord.

> *And the Lord said unto Satan, Hast thou considered my servant Job, that there is none like him in the earth, a perfect and an upright man, one that feareth God, and escheweth evil?* (Job 1:8)

Job was not perfect in the sense of being sinless, but in the sense that he was whole, that he was perfect before God. He was an extraordinary individual and the trials in his life where absolutely extraordinary as well. He was tried through the circumstances of his own life—the circumstances peculiarly his, the trials peculiarly his.

Every trial that you and I have is the same. Everyone's is. *We are tried through the circumstances of our lives.* Behind every circumstance of our lives, every situation, every trial, there is a definite, meaningful reason. Often we are not able to see that reason or comprehend it through our natural senses.

Man is not just a simple, single-cell being. He is a highly complex creature. He is a unique three-dimensional being made up of body, soul, and spirit. Man does not live in one world at a time; he lives simultaneously in two worlds. He lives in a natural world—a materialistic, human, flesh, bones and blood world. It is very real. Man also lives in a spirit or spiritual world. This is just as real as the natural world—in a sense, more so.

Job's trials in the circumstances of his life took place in both of his worlds. He was tried in the natural world, in his physical body and in the material realm, but his greatest test was his trial in the spiritual world, the world of his faith.

Job lost his wealth. He lost his property. He lost his children. He lost his physical health. He even lost the help and the sympathy of an understanding wife. Job's trials came so fast and furiously that they arrived one on top of the other. Before he could recover from one blow, another was delivered. While one messenger would be giving him a report of some loss, another would arrive with the story of an even greater loss. It was staggering.

In the natural, the events would have been completely shattering. But in the midst of it all, there was one thing that Job never lost. He never lost his faith in God! *"In all this Job sinned not, nor charged God foolishly"* (Job 1:22).

Unlike many of us, Job knew that this life consists of more than what we see or what we possess. He had confidence in God.

He knew God well enough that he was willing to place this seen life, these natural circumstances, completely in the hands of his heavenly Father.

Job knew that even if his eye never saw the truth, God's eye did. "I cannot see God," he confessed at one point. "I cannot feel Him, but it is all right, because,"

> *He knoweth the way that I take: when he hath tried me, I shall come forth as gold* (Job 23:10).

Job was a way-maker for us. At the time, he did not see the reasons behind his harassment by Satan, but it pleased God to lift the veil through the scriptures and let us see what was going on in the heavenlies, behind the scenes, in the trials of this righteous man. Job was having his battles in the natural, but it was really a spiritual battle. What was going on behind the scenes was a direct confrontation between God and Satan, with Job as the battleground.

It is very important for us to understand that God did not send Job's trial or Job's sufferings. God does not send afflictions upon the righteous, because He cannot go contrary to His Word or His will. He has said: *"...I am come that they might have life, and that they might have it more abundantly"* (John 10:10). God did not send Job's afflictions. There was a spiritual reason behind what people were able to see on the surface.

Yes, God permitted these afflictions for a reason. Permissively, God delivered Job into the hands of Satan. Completely unknown to Job, God was holding him up before Satan as an example of a good and just man.

> *And the Lord said unto Satan, Hast thou considered my servant Job, that there is none like him in the earth, a perfect and an upright man, one that feareth God, and escheweth evil?* (Job 1:8)

God loved Job. It was His plan and His desire to bless Job, to keep him, to prosper him. However, in order to prove what was in Job's heart, God permitted trials, tests, and reverses to come into

Job's life at the hand of Satan. God permitted Satan to test Job in the circumstances of his life, certain that Job would pass the test!

In the first two chapters of Job, we read all the adverse conditions and circumstances that had come into Job's life. Yet in every one of them, it was Satan who brought the problem, the sickness, the pain, the suffering—not God.

Behind every earthly trial there is a spiritual reason that man can never see with the natural eye. It takes the revelation of God to tear the veil away so that we can see the real root, the real cause, the real answer.

Even without seeing the battle in the heavenlies, Job had the key to victory—his faith in God. When Job won the battle, it was not so important what the results were in the natural world, but it was important that he won his victory in the spirit world. When he did, then the circumstances of his natural world were tremendously blessed. Everything fell into place.

Being able to see by the spirit what is behind our trials is the key to our victory in every situation and circumstances. Having thus located the real enemy, we can rise up in all the spiritual firepower God has provided for us and tear the victories that belong to God right out of the very hands of Satan.

## Discussion Questions

1. Have you ever experienced suffering (or seen others experience it) when there seemed to be no reason for it?
2. Is it easy or difficult for you to have faith when you don't understand why something is happening?
3. What is one truth from Job's story that you can apply to your own struggles?

### Note

1. "Why do the Righteous Suffer?" This is perhaps the most perplexing question any Christian ever has to face. My

book by that title answers that question which must be part of our spiritual strategy.

The book may be obtained by writing to: Morris Cerullo World Evangelism, P.O. Box 85277, San Diego, CA 92186. Enclosed with each book is an anointed prayer cloth. Use it as a point of contact. Place it upon your physical body wherever your sickness is.

There is no healing power in the cloth. The Bible says, *"If two of you shall agree on earth as touching any thing that they shall ask, it shall be done for them of my Father which is in heaven"* (Matthew 18:19). As you receive this anointed prayer cloth that I have personally prayed over, receive God's blessings for any needs you may have—physical, financial, or family problems. Remember there is no distance with God in prayer as we agree together. *You will find it works!*

CHAPTER 16

# SATAN IN THE AFFAIRS OF NATIONS

IT IS IMPORTANT AND NECESSARY to impress upon the spiritual warrior the very personal nature of spiritual warfare—Satan's hatred for every single soul on earth. It is also important to know that it is this same Satan who is behind the struggle between ideologies and nations today. It has always been that way, as he has sought to influence nations and leaders down through the ages.

Nowhere is Satan's hand more clearly seen than in the affairs of the nation of Israel, not only because of God's unique blessing on the Jew, but because this nation is the vehicle used to bring forth Jesus who will finally conquer Satan completely.

Satan also is at work among nations today, stirring hatreds and passions. His special hatred for Israel is still clearly discernible. Satan's hatred for Israel has been aimed at the nation as a whole, and also aimed at the messianic line through which God prophesied the Messiah would come. When Adam and Eve sinned, they received judgment and punishment from God, as did Satan himself.

Satan's punishment carried Adam's forgiveness (and all humankind's) with the first promise of the Deliverer to come:

> *And I will put enmity between thee and the woman, and between thy seed and her seed; it shall bruise they head, and thou shalt bruise his heel* (Genesis 3:15).

Scarcely had God's judgment been pronounced upon man, woman, Satan, serpent, and earth as a result of the first sin before Satan was at work in the affairs of the first family once again. With the lesson of Eden strong upon him, Adam without a doubt instilled in his sons a knowledge of God and His requirements. Yet look at what happened in the worship of these two men:

> *...Abel was a keeper of sheep, but Cain was a tiller of the ground. And in process of time it came to pass, that Cain brought of the fruit of the ground an offering unto the Lord. And Abel, he also brought of the firstlings of his flock and of the fat thereof. And the Lord had respect unto Abel and to his offering: but unto Cain and to his offering he had not respect. And Cain was very wroth, and his countenance fell. And the Lord said unto Cain, Why art thou wroth? and why is thy countenance fallen? If thou doest well, shalt thou not be accepted? And if thou doest not well, sin lieth at the door...* (Genesis 4:2-7).

Misunderstanding could not be the plea, for God clearly gave Cain another opportunity to do right. Nor can "thoughtlessness" or "convenience" be the excuse. The reason behind Cain's disobedience is revealed in its true light by the Holy Spirit in the New Testament: *"Not as Cain, who was of that wicked one, and slew his brother..."* (1 John 3:12). He was going through the motions of a form of worship to God, but he was really a servant of Satan.

> *Know ye not, that to whom ye yield yourselves servants to obey, his servants ye are to whom ye obey; whether of sin unto death, or of obedience unto righteousness?* (Romans 6:16)

Orders of the human race who came along after Cain entered into more open forms of Satan worship, embracing activities actually involving demon personalities. God's first commandment was that He alone was to be worshiped, but men continued to follow wickedness and God found it necessary to stress laws prohibiting Satan worship.

The reality of the existence of evil spirits by which Satan, their prince, carries out his evil work is clearly attested to by the witness of Moses. In the Law of Moses, which he wrote from the words which Jehovah God spoke to him on Mount Sinai, there is a clear definition of the activity of demons in human life. God calls this involvement "an abomination," which is a sin of the lowest degree.

> *When thou art come into the land which the Lord thy God giveth thee, thou shalt not learn to do after the abominations of those nations. There shall not be found among you any one that maketh his son or his daughter to pass through the fire, or that useth divination, or an observer of times, or an enchanter, or a witch, Or a charmer, or a consulter with familiar spirits, or a wizard, or a necromancer. For all that do these things are an abomination unto the Lord: and because of these abominations the Lord thy God doth drive them out from before thee. Thou shalt be perfect with the Lord thy God* (Deuteronomy 18:9-13).

God commanded that anyone who was polluted with these spirits of abomination should receive the death penalty. Christ took the death penalty for these as well as any other sins on the cross. If a person dealing with these things today will repent, God will forgive this sin and the person will be saved. Christ has paid the penalty for all sin for all those who believe in Him.

The words of Moses prove the existence of evil spirits, their activity, influence, and deception among men, their ability to communicate with and control human beings, and God's absolute hatred of these things. Would God give us laws to warn us against dangers which are imaginary, as some people say evil spirits are? Would God command the death penalty for dealing with "imaginary" forces?

When Moses and Joshua led the children of Israel, they strictly enforced the strong measures decreed by God against the activity of wicked spirits. Violators were put to death. After the deaths of

Moses and Joshua, much of Israel fell into darkness, brought about by the workings of evil spirits as the leaders of the people yielded to temptation. They began to commit the sins of idolatry, witchcraft, and other sins of the people around them.

## Attacks in the Old Testament

The finger of Satan at work in the affairs of Israel can be traced throughout the Old Testament. A prime example is to be found in the book of Numbers. God had mightily blessed Israel, so much so that His sign was unmistakably upon them before all the nations. They were so blessed in fact that the other nations feared them. To offset this fear, Balak, the king of Moab, sent for Balaam to come and curse the children of Israel.

> *He sent messengers therefore unto Balaam…saying, Behold, there is a people come out from Egypt: behold, they cover the face of the earth, and they abide over against me: come now therefore, I pray thee, curse me this people; for they are too mighty for me…* (Numbers 22:5-6).

Though he was offered riches and prestige, Balaam over and over declared that he was powerless to curse those whom God had blessed.

> *And Balaam answered and said unto the servants of Balak, If Balak would give me his house full of silver and gold, I cannot go beyond the word of the Lord my God, to do less or more* (Numbers 22:18).

A very real truth is contained in this: No one can put a curse where God has placed blessing. However, man still has the power of choice. When he chooses to leave the place of God's blessing, he makes himself completely vulnerable to Satan.

Though Balaam could not open his mouth and pronounce an effective curse on Israel, he did show Balak how to draw Israel away from the place of blessing by getting them to disobey God. What he did is revealed in the book of Revelation:

> *But I have a few things against thee, because thou hast there them that hold the doctrine of Balaam, who taught Balac to cast a stumbling block before the children of Israel, to eat things sacrificed unto idols, and to commit fornication* (Revelation 2:14).

By causing Israel to disobey God, Balaam, in effect, caused them to bring a curse upon themselves.

There is a story in the Old Testament of a man who was singularly blessed by God, who turned from God to the extent of actively seeking Satan's power. That man is King Saul, who had been chosen the first king of Israel. We can read this story in First Samuel.

There was a time Saul was anointed by God: *"And the spirit of God came upon Saul when he heard those tidings..."* (1 Samuel 11:6). By presumption and rebellion against God, Saul later became prey for demonic spirits.

> *But the Spirit of the Lord departed from Saul, and an evil spirit from the Lord troubled him* (1 Samuel 16:14).

When Saul persisted in his rebellious ways, he lost contact with heaven completely. Though one of his acts as king had been to outlaw witches (see 1 Samuel 28:9), he sought out a witch for help.

> *And when Saul inquired of the Lord, the Lord answered him not, neither by dreams, nor by Urim, nor by prophets. Then said Saul unto his servants, Seek me a woman that hath a familiar spirit, that I may go to her, and inquire of her. And his servants said to him, Behold, there is a woman that hath a familiar spirit at Endor* (1 Samuel 28:6-7).

Saul's path led continually downward and he committed suicide on the field of military defeat.

This is a great parallel to what is going on in spiritual realms today. A great hunger in the hearts of people for the supernatural is causing many who have no spiritual relation to God to turn to the occult.

Though David was described as a man after God's own heart (see Acts 13:22), he had lapses in which he yielded to Satan's influence. The best known occasion is his adultery with Bathsheba and the murder of her husband (see 2 Samuel 11).

On another occasion, it is recorded: *"And Satan stood up against Israel, and provoked David to number Israel"* (1 Chronicles 21:1). Upon each failure, however, David repented and found forgiveness and cleansing from God. (see Psalms 51).

In First Kings 22, we have God permitting an evil spirit to operate as a lying spirit in the mouths of King Ahab's prophets to lead the wicked king to his death on the battlefield. This story strongly points out that despite the extent of satanic activity, God is always in ultimate control and will bring His own purposes to pass despite anything Satan can devise. That is why the nation of Israel has been so miraculously preserved. Nothing else but the concerted efforts of Satan can account for the terrible hatred for and attacks upon Jews down through the years.

During the time of Queen Esther, Satan worked through the hatred of Haman to cause King Ahaseurus to enact a law that would have wiped out the Jews.

> *And the letters were sent by posts into all the king's provinces, to destroy, to kill, and to cause to perish, all Jews, both young and old, little children and women, in one day...* (Esther 3:13).

It was a time of great trial and perplexity, yet the godly Mordecai, Queen Esther's cousin, never lost sight of the fact that God would protect the race. He beseeched Esther to intervene for her people at the risk of her life. When she demurred, Mordecai asked her, "Who knows whether you are come to the kingdom for such a time as this?" But he assured her:

> *If thou altogether holdest thy peace at this time, then shall there enlargement and deliverance arise to the Jews from another place...* (Esther 4:14).

It was a time of great spiritual warfare. Esther called a fast and God moved miraculously to preserve the nation.

## THE BATTLE TODAY

The Jew remains a hated target of Satan. Though the Messiah already has come, the Jew plays such a prominent part in last-day prophecy that he is still a prime target for Satan-inspired forces.

Only Satan could have moved through Adolph Hitler to produce the kind of madness that caused him to try to annihilate the entire Jewish population of the world. With six million Jews consigned to the ovens of the Nazis, no one on the face of the earth would have given much chance for the nation of Israel at the end of the Second World War. Yet God not only preserved a remnant, He moved in such a mighty way that within a few short years they reclaimed their historic land and established a new nation which figuratively shook its fist in the face of a disbelieving world.

The battle that is still going on against Israel today, the hatred by the Arabs, the prejudice of other nations, is inspired by Satan. Satan knows that this is still a chosen people with a unique place in God's end-time plan.

God has never deserted the Jews, and He never will. As He preserved them in the time of Esther and in the time of Hitler, so He will continue His watchful care. In fact, God will use that very hatred to draw Israel's enemies to the great battle described in the 38th chapter of Ezekiel in much the way that the lying spirit brought about the defeat of Ahab as discussed in this chapter. Surely God "maketh even the wrath of man to praise Him" (see Psalms 76:10).

Another way in which God's watchfulness and care for Israel can be clearly seen is this: In every other case where there has been little or no intermarriage with other races, that race has diminished or died out completely. The Eskimo is such a case. Yet Israel has retained its purity as a race and continues to propagate and prosper in a miraculous manner. As the prophecies concerning the first coming of the Messiah have all been fulfilled, God has preserved the race so that each promise of the second coming and fulfillment of all things will be carried out just as He has said.

The Christian actively engaged in spiritual warfare needs to know the truth behind the nations and governments of this world. They are just as involved in spiritual warfare as individuals. That is why we are enjoined to pray for governments and leaders.

> *I exhort therefore, that, first of all, supplications, prayers, intercessions, and giving of thanks, be made for all men; for kings, and for all that are in authority…* (1 Timothy 2:1-2).

Praying Christians can move the hand of God in the affairs of nations, and often have. God has used this ministry in a marvelous way in that respect in North America and in other countries as well. Because Israel is such a targeted area for satanic activity, we need especially to hold this nation up in prayer: *"Pray for the peace of Jerusalem…"* (Psalms 122:6).

We thank God for the vital role He has given us in the prophetic last-day outreach to the Jew in which He has commissioned us to reach every Jew with the message of the Messiah. Today, when there is a new crisis every day somewhere in the world—many of them concerning Israel—the need is greater than ever before for God-fearing people who will pray in the spirit and do battle with the forces of evil for men and governments. The need is greater today than ever before—the need for consecrated men and women who will heed the call to holiness and go out in the Name of Christ to defeat Satan and all he stands for.

Because Satan is so active in nations today, we need to pray more than ever to see God's people take authority in the spirit world and turn their nations around for God. That is the purpose for which God has given us the School of Ministry, to raise up God's Victorious Army to take the world for Jesus Christ in our generation.

When Christ appeared in Israel, He recognized that the spiritual problems of the Jewish people were caused by satanic powers, and

He began to wage war against them uncompromisingly. Moses in the Old Testament was a parallel to Christ in the New Testament: Moses, the only man who knew God face to face; Christ, the only begotten Son of the Father, who always stood face to face with God in heaven. Each recognized the existence of Satan. Moses and Christ both knew the devil's power, but they did not let that stop their walk with God, or that of their disciples. They waged war against it.

One of the main reasons we are seeing such a flood tide of evil today is because with the passing of many of the saints who held a high standard against Satan in the past years, has come a lower standard with each succeeding generation. The world constantly is subjected to the efforts of Satan to lower spiritual and moral standards.

> *Now the Spirit speaketh expressly, that in the latter times some shall depart from the faith, giving heed to seducing spirits, and doctrines of devils* (1 Timothy 4:1).

For years, the forces of Bible-believing people stood out in their communities as bright and shining lights, a restraint to the evil that always threatened to take over. Now, "modern thought" has usurped power over lives to the extent that there is a permissive attitude toward these evil works at every level of education and government. God is demanding a renewed standard of holiness among His Church today before the Second Coming of our Lord.

*"Blessed are the pure in heart: for they shall see God"* (Matthew 5:8). This New Anointing message not only is a message of power, it is a message of holiness and purification: *"purify your hearts"* (James 4:8).

If we want to be vessels of God's power, the Bible says we must live up to His standards of purity: *"...be ye clean, that bear the vessels of the Lord"* (Isaiah 52:11). That exhortation in the Old Testament is just as real in our day, for evil is even more rampant in the age in which we live.

## Discussion Questions

1. Look back over some of the examples of Satan's attacks in the Old Testament. Can you see these tactics at work today, in the world or in your own life?
2. Choose a promise scripture from this chapter (or your own reading) and begin to pray against Satan's attack on the nations.
3. Where do you see the most need for "standard-bearers"? Where is God giving you a specific burden to pray against evil and live by His Word? (If you aren't sure He is, ask Him for one!)

Chapter 17

# SATAN'S ATTACK ON CHRIST, PART 1

One of Satan's chief reasons for attacking Israel was to try to prevent his Archenemy, Jesus, from ever being born. God's Holy Word contains infallible proof that Jesus Christ is who He said He is. The scriptures prophesy continually of the Messiah, when He would come, where He would come, the line from which He would come, etc. There are 333 definite prophecies in the Old Testament that clearly point to the Messiah. If even one of these prophecies failed, it would negate every one of them.

Satan knows these prophecies. He has known since the judgment at the Garden of Eden that One was coming who would defeat him and bruise his head. He has had knowledge of the Word of God down through the ages. The enmity that God pronounced between Satan and the seed of woman dates from Eden and has never diminished. It will continue until all spiritual warfare is ended and Satan meets his final end.

Since that first prophecy of a promised Redeemer in Genesis 3:15, there have been many more prophecies of the Messiah, and there have been many attacks on the Word of God seeking to negate those prophecies. Satan sought to kill the Messiah before He was ever born by preventing His coming in the way and manner prophesied. Satan launched one of his most determined attacks upon the lineage of the Messiah which God prophesied, attacking the prophecies which prove beyond a doubt that Jesus is the promised Messiah. If only Satan could make one word of God to fail, he would win. But he could not.

This attack on the line of Christ was launched in the very beginning, with the sons of Adam as the targets, when one son, Cain, killed the other, Abel. You can easily see the conflict here between good and evil. Abel was righteous (see Hebrews 11:4). Cain was of the "wicked one," or the devil (see 1 John 3:12). The result was Satan's attempt, through Cain, to wipe out the godly line to eliminate the Seed of woman which had been promised.

> *And Cain talked with Abel his brother: and it came to pass, when they were in the field, that Cain rose up against Abel his brother, and slew him* (Genesis 4:8).

Satan could have eliminated the progeny of Adam altogether; the battle would have been over right then and there. However, God raised up additional seed of the first family. With the birth of Seth came the re-establishment of the godly line.

The events surrounding the murder of Abel vividly depict the continuing attack of Satan on the godly line through which the Messiah was promised. If Satan could wipe out the line at any period in history, the victory would be his. On several occasions, he seemed for a time to have succeeded, yet God never lost control. He moved in marvelous and amazing ways to show His Word true and to preserve the godly seed from extinction.

## The Line of Kings

That the Messiah would come from the line of Judah was prophesied in Genesis 49:10, and that He would come from a kingly line was prophesied when as yet the nation of Israel had no king:

> *The sceptre shall not depart from Judah, nor a lawgiver from between his feet, until Shiloh come; and unto him shall the gathering of the people be* (Genesis 49:10).

> *He hath not beheld iniquity in Jacob, neither hath he seen perverseness in Israel: the Lord his God is with him, and the shout of a king is among them* (Numbers 23:21).

And after the kingly line was established, God used Nathan to utter this prophecy to David regarding his seed:

> *He shall build an house for my name, and I will stablish the throne of his kingdom for ever* (2 Samuel 7:13).

The history of the kings can be traced through the books of Kings and Chronicles. Though there was a division of the people into the children of Israel and the children of Judah, Judah remained the promised line. In these great books are the stories of many battles, much bloodshed and great intrigue which might be regarded as mere human history, but far from it. Spiritual warfare was continually at work.

At one point in history, Satan caused the entire promised kingly line of the Messiah to be completely annihilated, except for one small boy. God miraculously hid this child away, preserving the promised Seed.

> *And when Athaliah the mother of Ahaziah saw that her son was dead, she arose and destroyed all the seed royal* (2 Kings 11:1, see also 2 Chronicles 22:10).

If she had been successful, Satan would have succeeded in breaking the Word of God. Yet look at the ever-present protection of God:

> *But Jehosheba, the daughter of king Joram, sister of Ahaziah, took Joash the son of Ahaziah, and stole him from among the kings' sons which were slain; and they hid him, even him and his nurse, in the bedchamber from Athaliah, so that he was not slain. And he was with her hid in the house of the Lord six years...* (2 Kings 11:2-3, see also 2 Chronicles 22:11-12).

The line was preserved. Joash was put on the throne and reigned for 40 good years. Afterward, the line was continued through Amaziah, Uzziah, Jotham, etc., through Jehoiachin. Zedekiah was reigning at the time that Judah went into captivity in 586 B.C., and we read of him that his sons were slain before his eyes (see 2 Kings 25:7).

However, Zedekiah had a brother, Jeconiah, whose children included Salathiel. Salathiel and his son, Zerubbabel, were common links in the genealogies of both Joseph and Mary as outlined in Matthew 1 and Luke 3, respectively.

During the years of captivity, many records and genealogies were lost so that many of the priests were unable to trace that lineage to establish their right to the priesthood. However, God preserved the records of the Messiah's line, and so we have it presented to us today—a line that Satan could not eradicate.

## SATAN ATTACKS AGAIN

Unsuccessful in his attempts to annihilate the Jewish race or to interrupt the promised line of the Messiah, Satan never gave up. The birth of Jesus found him with another plan to thwart God's purpose—to kill the newborn Christ child by putting it in Herod's heart to murder all the babies in Bethlehem. This activity was prophesied in the Old Testament:

> *Thus saith the Lord; A voice was heard in Ramah, lamentation, and bitter weeping; Rachel weeping for her children refused to be comforted for her children, because they were not* (Jeremiah 31:15).

> *Then was fulfilled that which was spoken by Jeremiah the prophet, saying, In Ramah was there a voice heard, lamentation, and weeping, and great mourning, Rachel weeping for her children...* (Matthew 2:17-18; Rachel was buried in Bethlehem, see Genesis 35:19-20; 48:7).

The second chapter of the book of Matthew tells the story. When the wise men from the east inquired of Herod about the Child whose birth was signaled by the great star they followed, Herod was troubled. He encouraged the men to find the Child and to bring him word again, "*that I may come and worship Him also*" (Matthew 2:8).

His true purpose was revealed by God through a dream and the men returned home by another route. Herod then ordered the death of all children in Bethlehem under the age of two years. His wicked plan to kill the Christ at the cradle level failed when Joseph also was warned of God in a dream.

> *...The angel of the Lord appeareth to Joseph in a dream, saying, Arise, and take the young child and his mother, and flee into Egypt, and be thou there until I bring thee word: for Herod will seek the young child to destroy him. When he arose, he took the young child and his mother by night, and departed into Egypt* (Matthew 2:13-14).

The intense efforts of Satan to destroy the Child both before and after His birth were fruitless, of course. *"And Jesus increased in wisdom and stature, and in favour with God and man"* (Luke 2:52).

We know very little of Jesus's early years, but we do know that Satan continued to attack Him for the full course of His life on earth. After He was grown and His earthly ministry under way, we read such records as this:

> *And all they in the synagogue, when they heard these things, were filled with wrath, and rose up and thrust him* [Jesus] *out of the city, and led him unto the brow of the hill whereon their city was built, that they might cast him down headlong* (Luke 4:28-29).

Each time God preserved Jesus until the appointed time: *"But he passing through the midst of them went his way"* (Luke 4:30). Even though Jesus was a prime target for Satan's attacks, never once was He at Satan's mercy, and never once did He lose a battle.

## Discussion Questions

1. What are some of the promises God has given you?
2. Have you experienced Satan attacking you in order to prevent God's promises reaching fulfillment in your life?
3. Do you have a testimony of God fulfilling His word to you in spite of Satan's attacks? If not, do you know someone who does?
4. Satan had all of human history up to the birth of Jesus to prevent His coming, and he failed. How does this connect to your life and God's promises to you?

CHAPTER 18

# SATAN'S ATTACK ON CHRIST, PART 2

AS RAMPAGING AS HIS ATTACKS against Israel and the messianic line were, Satan's main satanic attack against Jesus as He began His earthly ministry was not one of overt violence, but of temptation. It is an example of utmost importance to us today from several perspectives.

If Satan fails to destroy from outside, with violence, he seeks to overthrow from inside, by temptation to disobedience to God. The Gospel of Mark has a very short account of the threefold temptation of Jesus Christ in the wilderness:

> *And immediately the Spirit driveth him into the wilderness. And he was there in the wilderness forty days, tempted of Satan; and was with the wild beasts; and the angels ministered unto him* (Mark 1:12-13).

Two other Gospels, however, give a much fuller account of the specific temptations which Jesus endured and overcame. These accounts are contained in the fourth chapters of Matthew and Luke.

During this time, Satan came at Jesus in three separate and distinct ways. One: Satan sought to get Jesus to turn stones into bread to satisfy His hunger following His 40-day fast. Two: Satan showed

Jesus the glories of the world which he offered to Him in exchange for His worship. (This was the second temptation in Luke's account, third in Matthew's.) Three: Satan took Jesus to the pinnacle of the temple and urged Him to jump in order to show His supernatural ability. (This is the second temptation in Matthew's account.)

Luke's account of these three temptations ends with this statement: *"And when the devil had ended all the temptation, he departed from him for a season"* (Luke 4:13). Matthew's account contains added information of great comfort: *"Then the devil leaveth him, and behold, angels came and ministered unto him"* (Matthew 4:11).

All truth is parallel. If you have not already done so, read the full account of this spiritual warfare between Satan and Christ in these two Gospels. How Jesus fought and prevailed is our example in overcoming Satan when we are tempted, for temptation to evil is one of the strongest devices Satan has. The temptations of Jesus show several methods Satan uses in attacking the people of God. It also shows how we may win the battle of temptation and put Satan to flight every time.

## Facing Temptation

No one is beyond temptation. No one is beyond attack by the enemy. We can be beyond defeat as Jesus was, but we are not beyond attack. As we learned in our study of Job, an attack by Satan is not a sign of sin or failure. It is a sign of the continuing warfare that assails every person who walks on this earth.

Although Jesus is divine, although He is God Incarnate, while here on earth He was also 100 percent man. In combating the temptations of Satan, He did not call upon any supernatural or divine power to which we do not have access. We have the same resources, the same strength, for fighting Satan and overcoming him that Jesus used when He won the victory.

Jesus was tempted in the three identical points in which Adam was tempted. These also are the same points which incorporate every type of temptation that comes to humankind. These three types of temptation outlined in the Bible are:

- lust of the flesh
- lust of the eyes
- and the pride of life

> *For all that is in the world, the lust of the flesh, and the lust of the eyes, and the pride of life, is not of the Father, but is of the world* (1 John 2:16).

No attack of Satan, no temptation, comes upon a child of God without the "foreknowledge" and the permission of God Himself, nor does it ever come without complete provision for victory.

> *There hath no temptation taken you but such as is common to man: but God is faithful, who will not suffer you to be tempted above that ye are able; but will with the temptation also make a way to escape, that ye may be able to bear it* (1 Corinthians 10:13).

During the temptation of Jesus, as in the case of Job, God knew exactly what was going on at all times. He was always completely in control. He is the One who made the rules and set the limitations. All of Satan's power is only allowed him by God, and it is always subject to God.

The temptation of Jesus differed somewhat from the trials of Job, in that Satan initiated the attack on Job while God deliberately led Jesus into the wilderness where His temptation came.

> *Then was Jesus led up of the Spirit into the wilderness to be tempted of the devil* (Matthew 4:1).

Mark used an even stronger word for the leading of Jesus into the wilderness arena. The wording in that Gospel is that *"the Spirit driveth Him into the wilderness"* (Mark 1:12).

It was a very necessary part of God's plan that Jesus endure the same kind of temptation which had overthrown the Edenic paradise.

It was only as Jesus was victorious where Adam had failed that it could be written: *"For as in Adam all die, even so in Christ shall all be made alive"* (1 Corinthians 15:22). It was only as Jesus suffered the same temptations that we suffer, and yet was without sin, that it could be written:

> *For we have not an high priest which cannot be touched with the feeling of our infirmities; but was in all points tempted like as we are, yet without sin* (Hebrews 4:15).

The warfare in all these points is still very real and very intense. If we follow the example of Jesus Christ, however, the outcome is never once in doubt. The temptations of Adam and of Jesus are full of parallels as well as contrasts. Satan seeks to come in unexpected ways in order to catch his victim off guard.

It was in the midst of plenty, with delicious fruit of every variety available to them, that Adam and Eve were tempted by Satan to eat the forbidden fruit of the Tree of the Knowledge of Good and Evil (see Genesis 3:1-6). It was following a 40-day fast when Jesus was hungry that Satan tempted Him with a plan for satisfying that hunger (see Matthew 4:2-4).

Satan comes against us with no pre-announced plan or pattern. He comes in times of blessing and in times of drought. He comes against the strong and the weak. He makes no allowances for physical condition, work load, home pressures, etc., but will rather use such situations to his own ends. Satan is never kind. He attacks young as well as old, strong as well as sick. His purpose always is to kill and to destroy.

Let us consider the temptations of Jesus one by one.

## LUST OF THE FLESH

> [Jesus] *Being forty days tempted of the devil. And in those days he did eat nothing: and when they were ended, he afterward hungered. And the devil said unto him, If thou be*

> *the Son of God, command this stone that it be made bread.* (Luke 4:2-3).

This temptation to the "lust of the flesh" (see 1 John 2:16), coincides with the serpent's temptation of Eve in which she *"saw that the tree was good for food"* (Genesis 3:6). Though Jesus was experiencing earthly hunger, He resisted all influence and direction from Satan. If Jesus called upon His innate deity to meet the test, He could not qualify as our High Priest:

> *For we have not a high priest which cannot be touched with the feeling of our infirmities; but was in all points tempted like as we are, yet without sin* (Hebrews 4:15).

It certainly was not wrong for Jesus to perform miracles, nor was it wrong for Him to eat food. It was wrong, however, for Him to move in any instance at the suggestion of Satan. He was led of the Spirit into the wilderness, and He continued to be led of the Spirit in every aspect of His life. Never once did Satan gain the slightest influence or control over Him whose life was without sin. *"For he hath made him to be sin for us, who knew no sin..."* (2 Corinthians 5:21).

God had not told Jesus to make bread of the stones. It was the Word of God in which He placed His reliance. That is why He could answer so unequivocally. Though Jesus Himself is the Living Word of God, He set the great example of overcoming temptation through the written Word of God.

> *And Jesus answered him, saying, It is written, That man shall not live by bread alone, but by every word of God* (Luke 4:4).

In this, as in the other two phases of the temptation, Jesus used the Word of God as His weapon. (For the effectiveness of this weapon, see chapter 23.) Adam and Eve could have stood fast upon the Word of God in the Garden. God's instruction to Adam had been very explicit:

> *...Of every tree of the garden thou mayest freely eat: but of the tree of the knowledge of good and evil, thou shalt not eat*

> *of it: for in the day that thou eatest thereof thou shalt surely die* (Genesis 2:16-17).

God's Word is very specific today regarding the lust of the flesh, yet man's wickedness is becoming greater and greater. The man or woman of God must combat the thought of lust at the very point of its "inception." God's Word as our defense and God's Spirit as our Guide should be the order of the day.

We know from First Timothy 4:1 that Satan is a seducing spirit. To yield to him one iota is to give him opening for greater inroads.

> *Now the Spirit speaketh expressly, that in the latter times some shall depart from the faith, giving heed to seducing spirits, and doctrines of devils* (1 Timothy 4:1).

Our weapon, as Christ's, must be this victory cry: *"Satan, it is written...."*

The second phase of Jesus's temptation was this:

> *And the devil, taking him up into an high mountain, shewed unto him all the kingdoms of the world in a moment of time. And the devil said unto him, All this power will I give thee, and the glory of them: for that is delivered unto me, and to whomsoever I will I give it. If thou therefore wilt worship me, all shall be thine* (Luke 4:5-7).

In coming to this earth as a babe and growing up as a Man, Christ willingly had left the glories of heaven which are far greater than the glories of all the kingdoms of the world. These glories were to be His again as well as all the glories of this earth, but not through an avenue that Satan could offer.

It is true that Satan has been permitted some power here on this earth, but at no time has he ever been given the dominion and power over this earth by God. As we studied earlier, Satan was given the dominion he has in the world by Adam who, in his disobedience to God, yielded himself to Satan. God had given the keys of dominion to Adam; Adam became the servant of Satan.

> *Know ye not, that to whom ye yield yourselves servants to obey, his servants ye are to whom ye obey; whether of sin unto death, or of obedience unto righteousness?* (Romans 6:16)

However, God is still in absolute control. He alone has the power over nations and governments. This reveals to us another great truth of satanic warfare as we study the temptation of Jesus: *Satan does not have the power that he claims to have.*

While it is true that he moves in and through people, including rulers, he is never the final authority. The promotion or fall of all men everywhere is only at the prerogative of God Himself. He alone is able to set up or pull down potentates.

> *For promotion cometh neither from the east, nor from the west, nor from the south. But God is the judge: he putteth down one and setteth up another* (Psalms 75:6-7).

> *...For there is no power but of God: the powers that be are ordained of God* (Romans 13:1).

Therefore, in the first place, the glories of this world were not Satan's to give, but God's. Secondly, while the devil was offering Jesus something that would be His in the future anyhow, he was suggesting that Jesus could bypass the pathway set out for Him by God and receive the rewards without the obedience.

Here again Jesus was our example of exact obedience to God's Word. The glory He received went far beyond any glory this world could offer.

> *And being found in fashion as man, he humbled himself, and became obedient unto death, even the death of the cross. Wherefore God also hath highly exalted him, and given him a name which is above every name: that at the name of Jesus every knee should bow, of things in heaven, and things in earth, and things under the earth; and that every tongue should confess that Jesus Christ is Lord, to the glory of God the Father* (Philippians 2:8-11).

Satan used lust of the eyes to weaken Eve in the Garden by showing her, not the glories of the world, but the pleasantness of the forbidden fruit.

## LUST OF THE EYES

*"And when the woman saw that the tree...was pleasant to the eyes..."* (Genesis 3:6). Seeing the forbidden fruit, the first couple coveted it and took it, their disobedience bringing the death that only Jesus's obedience under similar temptation could remedy:

> *For as by one man's disobedience many were made sinners, so by the obedience of one shall many be made righteous* (Romans 5:19).

Lust of the eyes is a favorite tool of Satan today. If he can cause the eye to look with longing upon the forbidden, covetousness enters the heart and leads eventually to all manner of gross sin—murder, theft, adultery, etc. Lust of the eyes is an area in which Satan is running rampant today, using every conceivable means to cause people to desire that which is not theirs, and go to great illegal and immoral lengths to acquire it.

Satan could not deliver what he did not possess to Jesus, and neither could he fulfill his promises to Eve. Neither can he deliver what he promises to man today. The things gained through lust and covetousness never satisfy no matter what Satan promises. Lust is insatiable.

> *Then when lust hath conceived, it bringeth forth sin: and sin, when it is finished, bringeth forth death* (James 1:15).

The time to quench the lust is at its very inception, and the way to quench it is the same method Jesus used for His victory:

> *...Get thee hence, Satan: for it is written, Thou shalt worship the Lord thy God, and him only shalt thou serve* (Matthew 4:10).

God is the only One who can deliver what He has promised. As we love and worship Him we find that *"godliness with contentment is great gain"* (1 Timothy 6:6).

The third temptation with which Satan confronted Jesus was this:

> *And* [Satan] *brought* [Jesus] *to Jerusalem, and set him on a pinnacle of the temple, and said unto him, If thou be the Son of God, cast thyself down from hence: For it is written, He shall give his angels charge over thee, to keep thee: and in their hands they shall bear thee up, lest at any time thou dash thy foot against a stone* (Luke 4:9-11).

In each of the three temptations, Satan used the word "if." In two of them the phrase was, *"If thou be the Son of God...."*

## PRIDE OF LIFE

The third temptation paralleled the third temptation of Eve and the third of the things John warned us as being among *"all that is in the world"*—the pride of life.

Eve's temptation to pride of life was Satan's promise: *"Ye shall be as gods."* Jesus's temptation was to here and now prove His deity to the world. This was neither God's time, nor God's method to show Christ's deity to the world at large. This was done through His resurrection and followed His painful death on the cross.

> *So also Christ glorified not himself.... Though he were a Son, yet learned he obedience by the things which he suffered; and being made perfect, he became the author of eternal salvation unto all them that obey him* (Hebrews 5:5,8-9).

The temptation to man today is to prove himself, his power, his superiority, his merit. It becomes the deflection of spiritual goals in a materialistic age.

Satan today uses the "if" in God's relationship to man to challenge acts presuming upon that relationship. However, our right relationship to God is based on our obedience to Him, not presumptuous insertion of our own wills. In this temptation, as in the others, Jesus used the Word of God as His authority and weapon: *"...it is said, Thou shalt not tempt the Lord thy God"* (Luke 4:12)

Though the entire incident is recorded in just a few short verses, there is no indication of how long the period of temptation lasted. We do know it followed a 40-day fast which, without a doubt, had left the physical body weak, but during which the spiritual Man was strengthened.

Two things happened here:

1. Effectively resisted by the bold use of God's Word, Satan fled.

2. God then sent His angels to minister to His Beloved Son.

Use of both of these spiritual weapons contributes to the victory that is ours when we follow Christ's example. Because He overcame, we can also, by the same means which He used. *"Submit yourselves therefore to God. Resist the devil, and he will flee from you"* (James 4:7). As Jesus submitted to God and resisted the enemy, Satan had no power over Him.

Jesus was not here for a holding mission. God sent Him here for far more than to withstand the devil. His warfare was far greater than that. Jesus's purpose for coming to earth was simply this:

> *...For this purpose the Son of God was manifested, that he might destroy the works of the devil* (1 John 3:8).

Jesus's purpose was to attack and destroy the enemy. Our purpose should be the same! *"...As my Father hath sent me, even so send I you"* (John 20:21).

To fulfill that purpose, let us analyze Satan's power and what, if any, effect or influence it can have over us. Do we have power that can disengage, defuse Satan's power over our lives and this world in which we live?

If all God's people lived in the Spirit and used the God-given power of the Holy Spirit to arrest the evil of Satan in their communities, it would not be long before an entire nation came under the influence of God, from every top government leader to housewives, laborers, attorneys, doctors, etc. Such a spirit of conviction of evil, wrongdoing, deceiving, and misleading would come that people would feel uncomfortable in their deceits.

## Discussion Questions

1. What does Satan most often use to tempt you—the lust of the flesh, the lust of the eyes, or the pride of life?
2. How can you make Jesus's responses your own as you resist Satan's attacks?

CHAPTER 19

# SATAN'S POWER IN LIVES TODAY

THE BIBLE CLEARLY STATES THAT Satan is real and that he exercises a certain amount of power in this world today:

> *Be sober, be vigilant; because your adversary the devil, as a roaring lion, walketh about, seeking whom he may devour* (1 Peter 5:8).

In addition to being known as the devil, Satan, and Lucifer, he is mentioned in the Bible as the dragon, serpent, adversary, Belial, Beelzebub, and others, at least 175 times. In Second Corinthians 4:4 he is referred to as the *"god of this world."*

Earlier, we discussed how he became the "god of this world." When Lucifer rebelled against God's will and was cast out of heaven (see Revelation 12:4), it was years before the birth of Jesus as a babe in Bethlehem. However, Christ was present during that judgment. Years later, He told His disciples: *"I beheld Satan as lightning fall from heaven"* (Luke 10:18).

When Satan was cast out, he set up his headquarters, established his armies, and began his all-out invasion of earth's atmosphere. The floodgates for Satan's power over humankind were opened by Adam in that first act of his obedience to Satan in the Garden of Eden.

> *Know ye not, that to whom ye yield yourselves servants to obey, his servants ye are to whom ye obey: whether of sin unto death, or of obedience unto righteousness?* (Romans 6:16)

It also brought judgment and death upon all humankind:

> *Wherefore, as by one man sin entered into the world, and death by sin; and so death passed upon all men, for that all have sinned* (Romans 5:12).

That is why man is degenerate from his youth. His basic nature is now sinful.

There are those who teach that "everyone is inherently good." An internationally known organization has as its slogan, "There is no such thing as a bad boy." Some put a label of "sickness" on such things as homosexuality, alcoholism, or other areas of bondage, but the Bible has this to say of fallen man:

> *The heart is deceitful above all things, and desperately wicked...* (Jeremiah 17:9).

> *Behold, I was shapen in iniquity; and in sin did my mother conceive me* (Psalms 51:5).

> *For there is not a just man upon earth, that doeth good, and sinneth not* (Ecclesiastes 7:20).

While the slogans and excuses invented by the world to accommodate their own deeds may sound pleasant to the ear, they simply are not true. Environment, training, social mores, etc. can cause people to exhibit civilized behavior, or "acceptable" habits and characteristics. However, the pull is always downward for the unregenerated person who has not been transformed by the new birth in Jesus Christ.

Several times in the Bible when days of real wickedness are described, the explanation is that:

> *...Every man did that which was right in his own eyes* (Judges 17:6).

> *And ye have done worse than your fathers, for, behold, ye walk every one after the imagination of his evil heart, that they may not hearken unto me* (Jeremiah 16:12).

Satan does not influence all people under his dominion to the same types of sin and degradation. In some instances he causes complete depravity, but many times works in and through those of great respectability and even those professing to be Christians. In any case, the heart of the unregenerate person is submission to the downward pull of sin: "*...his servants ye are to whom ye obey...*" (Romans 6:16).

That Satan has dominion and power over those who serve him is without dispute. This chapter, however, is not addressed to that fact, but to this question: How much power does Satan have over the life of a true born-again Christian?

One of the great paradoxes of Christian living is embraced in these two truths:

1. Satan was defeated by Jesus Christ in His death and resurrection. When we move into Jesus Christ through the new birth, we move into the Victor Himself. We become His servants. He becomes our Savior, our Victor, our Shield—the provision for every need that we have.

2. Satan does not acknowledge this defeat and moves against Christians with renewed effort and determination, seeking to destroy what he can before his final end.

> *The thief cometh not, but for to steal, and to kill, and to destroy...* (John 10:10).

We can read the Bible from beginning to end and back again and never find one single place where we are promised defeat in Christ Jesus. Every promise to the child of God is a promise of victory. Not just victory, but more than victory. We not only win the battle; we carry off the spoils of war and come from the battle with a great deal more substance than we had before the battle.

> *In all these things we are more than conquerors through him that loved us* (Romans 8:37).

That means that we have more than enough "goods" for the battle at hand, more than enough strength, more than enough power, etc. While we are not a match at all for Satan in our own strength, Satan is no match for us when we are in Christ. As we follow God's rules of spiritual warfare, not only must Satan flee from us, but he will end up in worse defeat than before he tried. It is only as we neglect or reject God's provisions and yield to Satan that he can lay one finger upon us.

When Satan came against Eve in the Garden of Eden, there was no way that he could force her to sin. He planted thoughts in her mind, he made suggestions, but it was only as she entertained these thoughts and yielded to the suggestions that sin entered the picture. She was not forced; she yielded. *"...She took of the fruit thereof, and did eat..."* (Genesis 3:6).

God sometimes allows Satan to exercise a certain amount of power over our circumstances, as in the case of Job. However, God had hedged Job with His love. Satan had to get permission from God for every assault he made against Job's circumstances. Nothing came into Job's life that had not passed before the loving Father—nothing! God allowed the circumstances to be touched, but God was always in control. He is always completely in control of our circumstances also.

There are two basic truths about all temptation that we need to know.

## Temptation Does Not Come from God

> *Let no one say when he is tempted, I am tempted of God: for God cannot be tempted with evil, neither tempteth he any man* (James 1:13).

God allows temptation to come into our lives for a reason—to prove us, to bring maturity to us, to prove Himself. We may not always know the exact reason, but there always is a reason. In Job's case, that which could be seen with the natural eye, that which Job could comprehend of the enemy's touch, was not what was really going on at all. What he could see and feel was a natural manifestation of something far deeper. What was really going on was spiritual warfare. This warfare, however, was completely limited in area, scope, severity, and time by God Himself. God was always in command.

Job, even without being able to comprehend his battle, maintained his integrity before God. He never lost his faith in God:

> *Though he* [God] *slay me, yet will I trust in him...* (Job 13:15).

> *But he knoweth the way that I take: when he hath tried me, I shall come forth as gold* (Job 23:10).

> *For I know that my redeemer liveth...* (Job 19:25).

He kept the victory of faith (spiritual), and he saw even greater victory in his natural circumstances, for we finally read:

> *So the Lord blessed the latter end of Job more than his beginning...* (Job 42:12).

If we could only see when Satan comes against us in any aspect of our lives—if we will just hold our integrity, keep our faith in God, use the weapons of our warfare He has provided—the battle is a spiritual battle between God and Satan, completely limited in scope by an ever loving Father, and it will last only as long as God permits. If we could only see that our battle is just:

From here ————————————————→ to here.

After that, more than victory. The Living Bible paraphrases Ephesians 6:13 this way: "*...and when it* [the battle] *is all over, you will still be standing up.*"

## Temptation Is Not a Sin

Temptation is not sin when it comes from an outside source and when it is rejected out of hand. It is only when it is tolerated and harbored that it becomes sin: *"But every man is tempted, when he is drawn away of his own lust, and enticed"* (James 1:14). The very first hint of temptation is the time for the Christian to act and to act decisively and effectively as Jesus did. If this is done, Satan has no power. He cannot force you to yield to sin. He cannot force you to sin. His only recourse is to flee.

Jesus used the same resources available to us with triumphant results. As we make use of the same resources in the same manner we have the same results—complete victory. Satan must leave and God Himself will minister to His own.

> *Submit yourselves therefore to God. Resist the devil, and he will flee from you* (James 4:7).

The devil must flee because not only does he have no power over us, but we have power over him—power given and delegated to us by Christ Himself.

> *Behold, I give unto you power to tread on serpents and scorpions, and over all the power of the enemy: and nothing shall by any means hurt you* (Luke 10:19).

The question no longer is how much power the enemy has over us—it is how much power we have over him!

> *Ye are of God, little children, and have overcome them: because greater is he that is in you, than he that is in the world* (1 John 4:4).

The circumstances that God permits Satan to shape in order to prove us become tools in God's hands for a greater abundance in our lives as we acknowledge him. *"Surely the wrath of man shall praise thee..."* (Psalms 76:10). Satan may try to cause our downfall, but God turns the test to His purposes and our good.

> *But as for you, ye thought evil against me; but God meant it unto good...* (Genesis 50:20).
>
> *And we know that all things work together for good to them that love God, to them who are the called according to his purposes* (Romans 8:28).

The answer to the question of this chapter, "How much power does Satan have over our lives?" is this—*None!* In Christ Jesus we have the power over Satan.

## Discussion Questions

1. Has there ever been a time when you believed God was tempting you?
2. Have you ever felt guilty after experiencing temptation, even if you did not give in and sin?
3. Has Satan ever tried to tell you that a "good Christian" doesn't feel tempted by the things you struggle with?
4. What can you start doing today to resist the devil and watch him flee from you?

Chapter 20

# THE CHRISTIAN AND DEMON POSSESSION

Satan himself is not omnipresent. Unlike God, he cannot be everywhere at once. He does, however, have legions and legions of evil spirit beings who do his work of binding and destroying humankind. Though many people today deny the reality of demon spirits or their activities in today's world, there are thousands of people who are dominated, influenced, controlled and directed by demons—and many who actually are demon-possessed.

From the Bible, we learn that demons can talk, using a person's lips and tongue. They can torment people and they themselves can be tormented. They can enter into people or animals. Demons can preach, tell lies, stand, walk, seek rest, and tell fortunes. They can deceive people and cause wrong decisions. They can cause blindness, deafness, and muteness, or bind a person with physical affliction. They can drive people fiercely, or lead them gently. They can cause people to commit suicide, or to be unreasonably jealous. They can cause people to be placed in asylums, or to rob and kill. In other words, just as good angels or spirits carry out the work of Christ in watching over and ministering to God's children, so do evil spirits seek to carry out the will of Satan here on earth.

Demon activity is an area people do not like to talk about. It is a negative. However, it takes positive and negative wires to produce light, and demon activity is an area where we must be knowledgeable. We not only must know the power of Satan as he comes against human lives, but we must know the power of God who is able to counteract every evil influence of the devil.

> *Ye shall know the truth, and the truth shall make you free* (John 8:32).

Many Christian leaders get nervous when you talk about demons. Someone said to me, "My church does not talk about demons. If you talk about demons, pretty soon you will be seeing them in the air." My response is this: If they are there, we had better see them. Also, we better know how to deal with them.

One of the most classic cases of demon possession in the Bible is the madman of Gadara whose story is told in Luke 8:27-36. (Also see Mark 5:1-15.) Demons were real more than 2,000 years ago, and they are just as real today.

## A Case of Possession

Several years ago, we were in a crusade in Pittsburgh, Pennsylvania when Satan tried to use a man in the congregation to disrupt our services. What happened is described by Rev. Mark Sutherland who was then pastor of Abundant Life Chapel, and later became associated in a key area with this ministry. Here is Rev. Sutherland's account of this incident:

> It was in the Pittsburgh crusade that I witnessed the most beautiful deliverance from demon possession.
>
> During the morning session, the pianist was playing, and Brother Cerullo was at the microphone on the platform.
>
> This huge man, 6 feet 2 inches, 240 pounds, approached the pianist and told him to play "Onward Christian Soldiers."

The pianist continued what he was already playing.

The man began to swing at Henry Davis (the pianist) and immediately a few of the men on the staff of World Evangelism ran to the front and grabbed the man to quiet him. They were all thrown to the floor.

Rev. Cerullo said, "Please take the man into one of the back rooms and minister to him."

The men, after much effort, were able to get him in the back room. He was very violent and super strong.

Upon entering the back room he kicked a rather sturdy chair. It broke into three pieces and went skidding across the floor.

In a moment's time there were seven ministers in a circle around the demon-possessed man. He was like a cornered animal. The ministers began to shout at him, "Come out of the man, you foul spirit. I command you, evil spirit, to come out now."

There was a moment's silence. The huge man quieted down, pointed to one of the ministers and said, "What is your name?"

The man proceeded to ask every pastor his name and then commanded each to sit down—which they did one by one.

I was the last one. When he asked me my name, I told him. He said, "Sit down."

I replied, "I'm not going to sit down. You are a lying devil and you are going to come out."

His countenance took on a very strange and stern look. He pointed his finger at me and said in a very dramatic gesture, "I am the Holy Spirit from heaven and because of your disobedience, I'm blotting your name out of the Lamb's Book of Life."

At this moment, Brother Cerullo and one of his associates came into the room. He said to his associate, "Please have all the men leave." I was allowed to stay.

Brother Cerullo walked up to this insane-acting man and quietly said, "Let's sit down." He sat down right in front of this large man, face to face.

The man reached over and took hold of Brother Cerullo's tie by the knot. He said to Brother Cerullo as he moved his tie from side to side, "Are you strong?"

The other associate and I were ready to run and help Brother Cerullo at the slightest motion from him.

Rev. Cerullo never raised his voice. He said quietly, "Yes, I am."

The man reached over and took Brother Cerullo's hand in the position of arm wrestling. He said, "I mean are you strong like this?" He began to move Brother Cerullo's arm back and forth. Brother Cerullo just let his arm relax. The man moved Brother Cerullo's hand back and forth a few times and then let go of it.

When he did this, Brother Cerullo just put his hand on the man's head and said, without raising his voice, "You foul unclean spirit, in the Name of Jesus, you come out of this man."

All of a sudden the man began to sob. Momentarily, he shook and sobbed and then he reached, weeping, put his arm around Brother Cerullo's neck and said, "I'm sorry."

They stood up, embraced and then Brother Cerullo took him by the hand and walked out the door through the crowd. What a trophy! What a deliverance!

> I observed the man many times after that in the hotel lobby, in the meetings, in the restaurants. He was set free and was perfectly normal. Obviously the power of the devil had been broken.
>
> I saw him singing, worshiping and praising the Lord in the services throughout the crusade.

We praise God for such deliverance as this. This is not some peculiar power that God gave Morris Cerullo or a few chosen people; it is a power that God wants all believers to possess. In fact, Jesus not only gave His disciples power over devils, He commanded them to have it:

> *And when he had called unto him his twelve disciples, he gave them power against unclean spirits, to cast them out, and to heal all manner of sickness and all manner of disease* (Matthew 10:1).
>
> *And as ye go, preach, saying, The kingdom of heaven is at hand. Heal the sick, cleanse the lepers, raise the dead, cast out devils: freely ye have received, freely give* (Matthew 10:7-8).

## Possessions in the Bible

Demons are disembodied spirits having no physical form, but they constantly seek beings to inhabit, human or animal. This habitation, or indwelling, is known as "demon possession," but demon spirits can also vex, oppress, or influence people from outside their beings. They attack man, seeking to destroy him mentally, physically, and spiritually. Here is the record of a woman who was bound physically by Satan.

> *And, behold, there was a woman which had a spirit of infirmity eighteen years, and was bowed together, and could in no wise lift up herself. And when Jesus saw her, he called her to him, and said unto her, Woman, thou art loosed from thine infirmity. And he laid his hands on her: and immediately she was made straight, and glorified God. ...And ought not this*

> *woman, being a daughter of Abraham, whom Satan hath bound, lo, these eighteen years, be loosed from this bond on the Sabbath day?* (Luke 13:11-13,16)

Because this woman was bound physically does not mean she was demon possessed, or that Satan had control of her soul. Jesus called her a "daughter of Abraham," indicating that she was a godly woman.

Others were vexed by spirits:

> *And, behold, a woman of Canaan came out of the same coasts, and cried unto him, saying, Have mercy on me, O Lord, thou Son of David; my daughter is grievously vexed with a devil* (Matthew 15:22).

A vexed person may be one who is disturbed, agitated, troubled, or afflicted physically, mentally, or both. Vexation usually begins as an outside force, but if not dealt with effectively, may become outright possession. The case referred to above is also described in Mark in this manner:

> *The woman was a Greek, a Syrophenician by nation; and she besought him that he would cast forth the devil out of her daughter* (Mark 7:26).

In this case the spirit was inside the person, as shown from Jesus's response to the woman's please:

> *And he said unto her, For this saying go thy way; the devil is gone out of thy daughter. And when she was come to her house, she found the devil gone out, and her daughter laid upon the bed* (Mark 7:29-30).

Though much demon activity comes from outside a person, it is true that spirits seek to enter a person and possess him. By possession we mean the act of possessing or owning. I do not believe that a blood-washed Christian can be demon possessed. Jesus and Satan cannot inhabit the same space. My Bible tells me:

> *Ye are of God, little children, and have overcome them: because greater is he that is in you than he that is in the world* (1 John 4:4).

I believe that if the enemy tries to get in, the Spirit of God will raise up a standard against him (see Isaiah 59:19). In temptation, Satan has no power over us but what we yield to him, and he certainly has no power to own a Christian. We are owned by Jesus Christ who bought us with His own blood.

> *What? Know ye not that your body is the temple of the Holy Ghost which is in you, which ye have of God, and ye are not your own? For ye are bought with a price: therefore glorify God in your body, and in your spirit, which are God's* (1 Corinthians 6:19-20).

There is no joint ownership or possession of people by God and Satan at the same time. However, it behooves us to keep ourselves under submission to God at all times, and our minds and hearts cleansed by the blood of Jesus.

## Our Mission

It not only is possible, but it is a must that we walk at liberty from the influence of Satan at all times, with every thought under subjection to Christ continually. It is not possible, however, to walk where we do not interface with people who have great problems and bondages in their lives. Neither do we wish to avoid them. God has commissioned us as His representatives here on earth to help such people: "*...As my Father hath sent me, even so send I you*" (John 20:21).

When Jesus was here on earth, He sent the 12 disciples forth to preach the Gospel of the kingdom, to heal the sick, and cast out devils. Later, He sent out 70 other disciples, two by two, who found that the power which they had been given worked. Jesus had power to set people free who were vexed and possessed of the devil, and when He sent His disciples forth, He delegated His authority to them.

> *After these things the Lord appointed other seventy also, and sent them two and two before his face into every city and place, whither he himself would come. ...And the seventy returned again with joy, saying, Lord, even the devils are subject unto us through thy name* (Luke 10:1,17).

There is one Bible story where a man, who was numbered neither with the 12 nor the 70, was casting out devils in the Name of Jesus:

> *And John answered him, saying, Master, we saw one casting out devils in thy name, and he followeth us: and we forbad him, because he followeth not us. But Jesus said, Forbid him not: for there is no man which shall do a miracle in my name, that can lightly speak evil of me* (Mark 9:38-39).

Paul was not numbered with the 12 or the 70, but years after Jesus ascended into heaven, this scene took place:

> *And God wrought special miracles by the hands of Paul: so that from his body were brought unto the sick handkerchiefs or aprons, and the diseases departed from them, and the evil spirits went out of them* (Acts 19:11-12).

Paul's anointing was such that evil spirits departed without his even being near the possessed person.

In one sense, only God has authority over devils. That authority was delegated to His Son Jesus.

> *And Jesus came and spake unto them, saying, All power is given unto me in heaven and in earth* (Matthew 28:18).

During His earthly ministry, Jesus commanded demons, unclean spirits, and disease to depart. They recognized His authority and were obedient to Him. Jesus has delegated that same authority to those who believe in His Name, that His work might continue here on earth.

> *Verily, verily, I say unto you, He that believeth on me, the works that I do shall he do also; and greater works than these shall he do; because I go unto my Father* (John 14:12).

Christ exercised no power that He did not make available to His followers. Each can know the power of God working and operating through him to cast out devils and to heal the sick. Not only do we have power over Satan in our lives and circumstances, but God gives us power to wade into Satan's territory to set other lives free from bondage.

> *Verily I say unto you, Whatsoever ye shall bind on earth shall be bound in heaven: and whatsoever ye shall loose on earth shall be loosed in heaven* (Matthew 18:18).

The delegation of God's authority to the followers of Jesus did not end with the first disciples. Every believer has a clear-cut authorization:

> *...Go ye into all the world, and preach the gospel to every creature. ...And these signs shall follow them that believe; in my name shall they cast out devils; they shall speak with new tongues; they shall take up serpents; and if they drink any deadly thing, it shall not hurt them; they shall lay hands on the sick, and they shall recover* (Mark 16:15,17-18).

With this authority, He has given us the weapons and the Word to bring His deliverance to the bound at their point of deepest need.

## Discussion Questions

1. Does Jesus's command to drive out demons apply to you today?

2. What would you do if confronted with a case like the man in this chapter? Would you be prepared to minister deliverance?

3. Why do you think God uses everyday people for wonderful works? Why do you think He wants to use you?

Chapter 21

# GOD'S ARMOR AGAINST SATAN'S ATTACK

Because of the peculiar nature of our enemy, the devil, God has provided peculiar armor for our protection and peculiar weapons with which to battle him.

We have pointed out that there are only two sides in this warfare that deal with all of life, and we have emphasized that this is a spiritual battle. We also have emphasized that the outcome is never in doubt. God has all power and all things are under His control, and we are victors because of Him. Satan has no power over us at all.

This is contingent, however, on one thing: *We must fight by God's rules.* He has not left us in doubt of these rules. He has made every provision for our welfare in battle, our growth even in the midst of the warfare, and for our ultimate and complete triumph over all the forces of the devil.

What most people are prone to forget is the purely spiritual nature of the proceedings. Sometimes we allow ourselves to be drawn into conflicts with people, or with things, or even with ourselves. Second Timothy 2:25 speaks of *"those that oppose themselves."* When we forget who the real enemy is, we misdirect our firepower and it is dissipated without really getting to the root of the problem at hand.

God has carefully outlined a complete set of armor for our protection and use in the battle and has set these forth in Ephesians 6:

> *Put on the whole armour of God, that ye may be able to stand against the wiles of the devil. For we wrestle not against flesh and blood, but against principalities, against powers, against the rulers of the darkness of this world, against spiritual wickedness in high places. Wherefore take unto you the whole armour of God, that ye may be able to withstand in the evil day, and having done all, to stand. Stand therefore, having your loins girt about with truth, and having on the breastplate of righteousness; and your feet shod with the preparation of the gospel of peace; above all, taking the shield of faith, wherewith ye shall be able to quench all the fiery darts of the wicked. And take the helmet of salvation, and the sword of the Spirit, which is the word of God: praying with all prayer and supplication in the Spirit...* (Ephesians 6:11-18).

The reason we must put on the whole or entire armor of God is very simple: In ourselves we are no match for the devil at all. Not the slightest. It is only in the strength of God that we can even stand. We must take our place in His complete protection and not leave one spot uncovered for Satan's touch. *"Neither give place to the devil"* (Ephesians 4:27)

Completely armored by God, however, we will stand in complete invulnerability to Satan's attack. *"...When it is all over, you will still be standing up"* (Ephesians 6:13 TLB). We must use every bit of the armor that God has given us so that not one spot is vulnerable to the attack of the enemy in any form.

Here is the armor God has provided us:

1. Having your loins girt about with truth

2. The breastplate of righteousness

3. Your feet shod with the preparation of the Gospel of Peace
4. The shield of faith
5. The helmet of salvation
6. The sword of the Spirit, which is the Word of God

Let us examine this armor one piece at a time.

## Your Loins Girt About with Truth

Truth is our undergirding. Though antagonists in many worldly battles and disagreements fight with lies, bluffing, exaggeration, and evasion, our undergirding is ever the truth of God's Word. Not only is His Word true, but He is Truth. Jesus said: *"I am the way, the truth, and the life..."* (John 14:6).

Since Jesus and Satan are opposites, it is safe and true to say that as Christ is the way, Satan is the wrong way. As Jesus is the truth, Satan is a liar and the father of lies. As Jesus is the life, Satan is the bearer of spiritual death.

> *Ye are of your father the devil, and the lusts of your father ye will do. He was a murderer from the beginning, and abode not in the truth, because there is no truth in him. When he speaketh a lie, he speaketh of his own: for he is a liar, and the father of it* (John 8:44).

If we make use of lies, we are using Satan's own tools, and certainly we are no match for him in that respect. Jesus is truth. We need never be afraid of truth, and we need never be afraid of truth failing us in any way. We can stand on any promise of God with unwavering faith that what He has promised, that will He do.

> *For all the promises of God in him are yea, and in him Amen, unto the glory of God by us* (2 Corinthians 1:20).

> *Blessed be the Lord, that hath given rest unto his people Israel, according to all that he promised: there hath not failed one*

> *word of all his good promise, which he promised by the hand of Moses his servant* (1 Kings 8:56).

In order to be girt with the truth, we must know the truth. We not only must know Jesus as the personification of Truth, but the whole Word of God as truth. There is no way to stand on what God has said if we do not know what He has said. Therefore, a personal knowledge of the Truth, Jesus Christ, and a knowledge of God's written truth are essentials in the battle at hand.

Satan is a wonder-worker and is capable of performing lying wonders designed to turn souls away from the truth. Those who do not love and hold to the truth are open to the snares of Satan and are destined for failure.

> *...The working of Satan with all power and signs and lying wonders, and with all deceivableness of unrighteousness in them that perish; because they received not the love of the truth, that they might be saved. And for this cause God shall send them strong delusion, that they should believe a lie: that they all might be damned who believed not the truth, but had pleasure in unrighteousness* (2 Thessalonians 2:9-12).

King Ahab fell into the snare of satanic delusion because he continually had shunned the truth of God. Those who do not love the truth, or do not want the truth, are defeated before the battle is begun. Truth is our only sure footing.

## The Breastplate of Righteousness

Righteousness goes hand in hand with truth, as in the passage from Second Thessalonians quoted above. Righteousness, as a breastplate, speaks of guarding the heart against all unrighteousness. Right standing before God is essential to the flow of His power in our lives.

There have been many cases where people of impure motives have sought to use the power of God without being qualified to use it. Those who attempt such folly not only will fail to obtain the desired results, but will run into serious difficulties because of their efforts to do so.

In Acts 19, we read of the seven sons of Sceva:

> *Then certain of the vagabond Jews, exorcists, took upon them to call over them which had evil spirits the name of the Lord Jesus, saying, We adjure you by Jesus whom Paul preacheth. And there were seven sons of one Sceva, a Jew, and chief of the priests which did so. And the evil spirit answered and said, Jesus I know, and Paul I know; but who are ye? And the man in whom the evil spirit was leaped on them, and overcame them, and prevailed against them, so that they fled out of that house naked and wounded* (Acts 19:13-16).

These men went through the same actions they had seen Paul go through, and used the same type of words which Paul had spoken. They even used the Name of Jesus. However, Satan knows when we are not shielded with the spiritual breastplate which guards our hearts. The battle went against the sons of Sceva, and they were forced to flee in wounded dishonor.

Another instance occurred when Simon, who had been a sorcerer, saw the power of the Holy Spirit in the lives of the apostles, and sought to purchase that power for himself:

> *And when Simon saw that through the laying on of the apostles' hands the Holy Ghost was given, he offered them money, saying, Give me also this power, that on whomsoever I lay hand, he may receive the Holy Ghost* (Acts 8:18-19).

Peter's scathing denunciation was:

> *...Thy money perish with thee...for thy heart is not right in the sight of God. ...I perceive that thou art in the gall of bitterness, and in the bond of iniquity* (Acts 8:20-21,23).

We realize that our own righteousness is of no avail. Yet we must enter into the righteousness that is in Christ Jesus if we are to utilize His power.

> *But we are all as an unclean thing, and all our righteousnesses are as filthy rags...* (Isaiah 64:6).

> *If ye abide in me, and my words abide in you, ye shall ask what ye will, and it shall be done unto you* (John 15:7).

It is impossible to walk in the Spirit of God if we are under condemnation.

> *There is therefore now no condemnation to them which are in Christ Jesus, who walk not after the flesh, but after the Spirit* (Romans 8:1).

While being careful that Satan not cause us to unjustly condemn ourselves, or that we fail to forgive ourselves for past wrongs for which God has forgiven us, we must also be careful that we walk in such a way that we do not bring real condemnation upon ourselves. When we do fail God, we must seek restored communion with Him and righteousness in Him at once.

> *If we confess our sins, he is faithful and just to forgive us our sins, and to cleanse us from all unrighteousness* (1 John 1:9).

## THE PREPARATION OF THE GOSPEL OF PEACE

This preparation is exactly what you are doing as you study this text. That this admonition is connected with the feet shows willingness, even eagerness, to go. Jesus's last command to His disciples before His ascension was: "*...Go ye into all the world, and preach the gospel to every creature*" (Mark 16:15). The preparation of the gospel of peace even makes our feet beautiful:

> *How beautiful upon the mountains are the feet of him that bringeth good tidings, that publisheth peace; that bringeth good tidings of good, that publisheth salvation; that saith unto Zion, Thy God reigneth!* (Isaiah 52:7)

Having the power of God will profit no one—neither yourself, God, nor the person in need if you do not obey Christ's command to "go."

Because many people have misinterpreted the "go," they have misdirected their efforts, not realizing that all can fulfill this command. Many are not called to go to foreign fields, or even to leave their hometowns, but every child of God is called to go into all the world of their own influence to spread the Gospel of Peace with which we have been prepared and shod.

Whatever your sphere of influence—whether you are a housewife, a professional person, or a laborer—be ready and prepared to go share the power of God in your life with others who need your ministry.

## THE SHIELD OF FAITH

Paul said that "above all" this is to be part of our armor. *"But without faith it is impossible to please him..."* (Hebrews 11:6). Without faith, we have no hold on the truth. Without faith, we cannot appropriate the righteousness that is in Jesus Christ. Without faith, we cannot shod ourselves with the preparation of the Gospel of Peace.

It is easy to see how important faith is when we consider again the case of Job. Under fiery attack by Satan (though unknown to him), Job lost everything that he had except his faith. *"Though he slay me, yet will I trust him..."* (Job 13:15). Job's faith held out until every one of Satan's fiery darts had hit against it and fallen away. Job not only remained unharmed, but was left in far better circumstances than he had been before those darts were fired at him. Faith not only quenches the fiery darts of the enemy sent against us, but equips us to send our fiery weaponry against him, since by faith in Christ we are enabled to do exploits for Him.

Peter was just one of the apostles who had a ministry of miracles, yet Peter attributed all his power where it rightfully belonged:

> *...Why look ye so earnestly on us, as though by our own power or holiness we had made this man to walk? ...And his name through faith in his name hath made this man strong, whom ye see and know: yea, the faith which is by him hath given*

> *him this perfect soundness in the presence of you all* (Acts 3:12,16).

For greater emphasis on faith and how to achieve it in your life without struggling, see my textbook on *Proof Producers,* the official textbook of the School of Ministry.

## The Helmet of Salvation

A helmet offers protection for the head. Our armor is not only righteousness, which is of the heart, but a mind that knows the salvation of God and is submitted to Him. The mind that is not stayed upon God becomes a playground for Satan's suggestions to pull us away from the truth into areas of wrong decisions and actions. Our minds continually must be under the blood of Jesus, which saved us from sin in the first place.

> *For God hath not given us the spirit of fear; but of power, and of love, and of a sound mind* (2 Timothy 1:7).

A person who dwells on negatives will never amount to a positive power force for God. God Himself has told us what kind of thoughts we must hold:

> *Finally, brethren, whatsoever things are true, whatsoever things are honest, whatsoever things are just, whatsoever things are pure, whatsoever things are lovely, whatsoever things are of good report; if there by any virtue, and if there by any praise, think on these things* (Philippians 4:8).

## The Sword of the Spirit

Truth not only is our standing place, it is our defense to cut down the attacks of the enemy when he comes against us. It is also our offensive weapon to cut into Satan's very territory. We are completely safe and sheltered in God for:

> *No weapon that is formed against thee shall prosper; and every tongue that shall rise against thee in judgment thou*

> *shalt condemn. This is the heritage of the servants of the Lord, and their righteousness is of me, saith the Lord* (Isaiah 54:17).

Clothed in the full armor of God, prepared to stand despite the battle, we move on in our warfare from defensive to offensive to learn how to invade Satan's territory and come away with unspeakable spoils of triumphant battle!

## Discussion Questions

1. Which parts of the armor of God are you clothed in?
2. Which parts are you missing, or only wearing sometimes?
3. How can you make sure that you are suited in the full armor of God?

CHAPTER 22

# WEAPONS OF OFFENSIVE WARFARE, PART 1: INTERCESSORY PRAYER

WHEN WE PUT ON THE whole armor of God and keep it intact in our lives, we have an impenetrable shield from every attack of the enemy, absolutely invulnerable. We thank God for it. However, that is far from all that God means for us to have. We are not in a holding maneuver. We are in an all-out war.

There is a great difference between a defensive battle and an offensive battle. In the sport of football, the rules note the two differing types of battle to the extent that one team is sent in for defensive play, and an entirely different one for offensive play.

In the natural warfare, there is a vast difference in the categorization of weaponry. We have defensive weapons such as nuclear bombs which are capable of annihilating millions of people at one time. Our treaties with foreign nations make allowances for different types of weaponry. We once had a treaty, for instance, which allowed the Russians to send defensive weapons to Cuba, but it was a violation of Russia's treaty with us if they sent offensive weapons there.

In the spiritual world, our military Leader is Christ Himself. He has provided us not only with defensive armor; He has provided us with the greatest, most potent weapons for offensive warfare into Satan's strongholds. Our warfare is of such far greater import than football as to make it a ridiculous parallel, but we can use it to point out a very great truth.

God's "team" is not divided into defensive and offensive squads. God does not mean for some of us to be defensive fighters and some to be offensive. He wants all of us to have on His whole defensive armor at all times, and it is His command that we take offensive action to invade Satan's territory and tear the spoils of battle from his hand, that we be more than conquerors (see Romans 8:37).

If I had my way, I would see that the song "Hold the Fort" was taken out of every hymnal. God does not want us just to "hold the fort." We will never win the battle "holding the fort." We win the battle by going into the devil's territory and tearing from his grasp the things that belong to the children of God and to the kingdom of God.[1]

## GOD-GIVEN STRATEGY

During the Vietnam War, I went to the battlefield to speak to the American troops. There I met with General William Westmoreland, commander of our forces. I asked him, "General Westmoreland, we have such tremendous forces in the United States of America; why can't we get in and win this war?"

The General replied, "Dr. Cerullo, we are not here to win the war, as such. We are here to try to stabilize the people of South Vietnam, then to pull out and let them handle the situation."

I knew from that statement that it was totally impossible for us to win the war in Vietnam. Why? Because it was a holding maneuver. It was not a war for victory. That is why there are so many perplexing areas in the world today. So many battles have been holding battles and they never resolve anything.

The Korean conflict was never resolved. Our troops were not allowed to penetrate beyond the 38th parallel. That meant enemy troops could come over the line, strike, and run back to their place of safety.

In Vietnam, the North Vietnamese guerrillas would find sanctuary in Cambodia, where our forces were forbidden to go. They would cross the line and strike at South Vietnam, and then flee back to their sanctuary. Our forces did penetrate into Cambodia to strike at the enemy on one occasion, but that was about the only offensive our forces took militarily in the entire time of our involvement in that country.

I am not debating the pros or cons of those wars. I am saying that such tactics will never bring victory. Neither will it in spiritual warfare! We have no right to go to war unless we mean to press on to victory.

God means for us to hold on. He means for us to persevere. He means for us to quench all the fiery darts of the enemy with our shields of faith. But he never meant for His blood-washed, sanctified, Spirit-filled children to quiver behind the lines of a spiritual "38th parallel."

God has called us to an Army. Militant. Mobilized. Moving. Making inroads into the very territory of Satan with no quarter given. We must remember at all times, however, that this is a purely spiritual battle. Our defensive weaponry, which we have already studied, is totally spiritual in nature. It is a shame that so many natural warfares are waged in the name of spiritual causes—the Christians and the Moslems who fought in Lebanon, the Israelis and Palestinians, the Catholics and the Protestants fighting in Ireland, the so-called Holy wars of the ancient crusades.

The real battle of the true Church is totally, purely spiritual in scope. The battles in your home or on your job, anywhere in your area of involvement should not be fisticuffs, guns, knives, or even railing. Our battle is not with flesh and blood. It is not with a wife or a husband. It is not with our children. It is not with a boss or a fellow-employee. Our battle is with our spiritual enemy, Satan.

Just as our defensive armor, which we have already studied, is totally spiritual, our offensive weaponry is totally spiritual. We can save ourselves a lot of hard lessons, and we can save our testimonies a lot of criticism if we keep this clearly in view. Many "messes" have been made, even in the ministry, by people who have taken matters into their own hands to try to "set things right." Often violence has occurred because of this.

We must be violent, all right, but not violent to people. We are to do violence to Satan's forces in the spirit world. Certainly his forces seek to do violence to us and to the kingdom of God. To seize the keys of dominion back from Satan, we must be violently determined in the spirit.

> *And from the days of John the Baptist until the present time, the kingdom of heaven has endured violent assault, and violent men seize it by force [as a precious prize—a share in the heavenly kingdom is sought with most ardent zeal and intense exertion]* (Matthew 11:12 AMP).

Our violence is never in the natural arena at all, and neither are our weapons.

> *For though we walk in the flesh, we do not war after the flesh: (for the weapons of our warfare are not carnal, but mighty through God to the pulling down of strong holds;) casting down imaginations, and every high thing that exalteth itself against the knowledge of God...* (2 Corinthians 10:3-5).

How can we be violent in the spirit? What are our violent weapons?

We have a number of spiritual weapons, yet all operate as a single powerful unit that rolls to victory every time they are scripturally utilized. Though we will try to consider these weapons one at a time, they are all intricately interwoven and all are necessary to our overwhelming victory over the things of Satan.

Using the military as a parallel, we might say that we are the Army of God, the infantry, the land Army, marching to victory in the Name of Christ. We might say that those who sail to other lands to carry the message of the resurrected Christ are the Navy, traveling to foreign ports. However, the real power is the power of the Air Force over us all which penetrates and wipes out the enemy. This powerful air force is composed of these irresistible weapons—prayer, fasting, and the Word of God.

## FIGHTING WITH PRAYER

When I speak of prayer as an offensive weapon, I am not talking about the kind of praying that we normally do at the breakfast table, in our five-minute devotions, or in Sunday school. All sincere prayer to God is good and has its place. Paul tells us we must *"Pray without ceasing"* (1 Thessalonians 5:17). We can and we should remain in an attitude of prayer and praise at all times, ever mindful of the blessings and protection of God.

However, the prayer that is our offensive weapon is the travailing, prevailing, wrestling of the spirit that turns men and nations around for God. The violence of this type of prayer is exemplified in our record of the prophet Daniel.

> *In those days I Daniel was mourning three full weeks. I ate no pleasant bread, neither came flesh nor wine in my mouth, neither did I anoint myself at all, till three whole weeks were fulfilled.…And, behold, an hand touched me, which set me upon my knees and upon the palms of my hands. …Then said he unto me, Fear not, Daniel; for from the first day that thou didst set thine heart to understand, and to chasten thyself before thy God, thy words were heard, and I am come for thy words* (Daniel 10:2-3,10,12).

Here were spiritual forces at war, and what a battle it was. Daniel was praying and seeking God in the manner which was his custom:

> *And I set my face unto the Lord God, to seek by prayer and supplications, with fasting, and sackcloth, and ashes* (Daniel 9:3).

It was because of such seeking after God that God revealed so much to Daniel and used him in such an outstanding way. It was a violent time in Daniel's life when he was thrown to the lion's den (see Daniel 6). Where was the violence? Daniel was not harmed.

The violence had already been done in the spirit world through Daniel's prayer life. The lions could not open their mouths. It was not that the lions were not violent; they killed the men who accused Daniel before they even reached the bottom when the king had them thrown into that same lions' den. The lions could not touch Daniel because his warfare had taken place in the spirit world. The battle had been won spiritually. When that was done, the answer came in the natural world. The natural order of things favored Daniel.

The Scripture quoted above gives a graphic look behind the scenes at Daniel's prayer life. He sought God for three full weeks before the answer came. Yet the heavenly messenger told him his prayer was heard the very first day. There was a battle going on behind the scenes. Evil forces withstood God's heavenly messenger, but Daniel continued to pray, and God continued to send help.

God has far greater forces on His side than Satan has on his. God will always win. We can count on it. We can count it done. God hears us the very first day, the very first minute that we set ourselves to seek Him. The answer must come as we persevere in prayer.

A line from Alfred Lord Tennyson that is widely quoted says, "More things are wrought by prayer than this world dreams of." This is true, because there are some individuals—not many, but some—who see the real power of prayer in the affairs of men and nations. Far too many people, Christians even, have a fatalistic approach to problems. They say, "What will be, will be." They fail to see how prayer mightily moves the hand of God and tears down the very strongholds of Satan.

Understand that when we pray, God is not our adversary. Satan is our adversary. Intercessory prayer is the force that brings God and all His resources (which are immeasurable, unlimited) to our side to effect the victory. It is the weapon God gave us with which to take the limit off Him and cut Him loose to work in our lives in a miraculous way.

To those who find the dynamic secret of intercessory prayer, it becomes a lifetime calling. To others, motivated by extreme pressure, need, or desire, it may be a one-time experience for meeting the need of the moment only. However, this instrument is so powerful, so effective, so guaranteed by God Himself that at one time Isaiah found God to be surprised that there was no one making use of this powerful means of bringing God down to man to meet man's most vital needs.

> *And* [God] *saw that there was no man, and wondered that there was no intercessor...* (Isaiah 59:16).

Job, in his extremity, used a term that well describes the intercessory prayer warrior.

> *Neither is there any daysman betwixt us* [between God and Job], *that might lay his hand upon us both* (Job 9:33).

In the ultimate, of course, Jesus Himself is our Daysman.

> *...It is Christ that died, yea rather, that is risen again, who is even at the right hand of God, who also maketh intercession for us* (Romans 8:34).

However, God has placed it within the scope of our ability and the scope of our responsibility for us to be daysmen, by the fervor of our prayers reaching out in spirit to touch both God and man, bringing them together for that tremendous touch whereby another need is met miraculously.

We may make intercession for our own needs, such as Hannah did in First Samuel 1. Unable to bear children, Hannah went to the temple on her own behalf and sought God so desperately that the priest at first thought she was drunk. To him, Hannah explained the condition of her heart and spirit.

> *And Hannah answered and said, No, my lord, I am a woman of a sorrowful spirit: I have drunk neither wine nor strong drink, but have poured out my soul before the Lord. Count not thine handmaid for a daughter of Belial: for out of the abundance of my complaint and grief have I spoken hitherto* (1 Samuel 1:15-16).

God saw the anguish of Hannah's heart and the sincerity of the request, and He gave her the desire of her heart to give her a miracle son.

> *Wherefore it came to pass, when the time was come about after Hannah had conceived, that she bare a son, and called his name Samuel, saying, Because I have asked him of the Lord* (1 Samuel 1:20).

God was so moved by Hannah's prayer that Samuel, as she named her first child, was not the only result of her travail. She was more than a conqueror in her battle.

> *And the Lord visited Hannah, so that she conceived, and bare three sons and two daughters...* (1 Samuel 2:21).

## Great Intercessors

The greatest use of intercession is that in which we in total selflessness penetrate the heavens for the needs of others with no regard for our own position and no desire for rewards. Such an intercessor was Moses. On one occasion, Moses stood in the gap for Israel, which had come under God's wrath:

> *And Moses besought the Lord his God, and said, Lord, why doth thy wrath wax hot against thy people, which thou hast brought forth out of the land of Egypt with great power, and with a mighty hand? Wherefore should the Egyptians speak, and say, For mischief did he bring them out, to slay them in the mountains, and to consume them from the face of the*

> *earth? Turn from thy fierce wrath, and repent of this evil against thy people. Remember Abraham, Isaac, and Israel, thy servants, to whom thou swarest by thine own self, and saidst unto them, I will multiply your seed as the stars of heaven, and all this land that I have spoken of will I give unto your seed, and they shall inherit it for ever* (Exodus 32:11-13).

God was so angry at rebellious Israel that He threatened to annihilate them completely and start a new family from Moses. Moses was more concerned with the needs of the people than he was with the honor of being the father of a new seed. He interceded for them with great fervor of heart.

> *And Moses returned unto the Lord, and said, Oh, this people have sinned a great sin, and have made them gods of gold. Yet now, if thou wilt forgive their sin; and if not, blot me, I pray thee, out of thy book which thou hast written* (Exodus 32:31-32).

Moses' prayers stayed the hand of God's judgment on that nation.

Through intercessory prayer, we may have mastery and dominion over the very elements of nature. A precedent for this is to be found with Elijah in his prayer for rain after three years of drought.

> *...And Elijah went up to the top of Carmel; and he cast himself down upon the earth, and put his face between his knees, and said to his servant, Go up now, look toward the sea. And he went up, and looked, and said, There is nothing. And he said, Go again seven times. And it came to pass at the seventh time, that he said, Behold, there ariseth a little cloud out of the sea, like a man's hand. And he said, Go up, say unto Ahab, Prepare thy chariot, and get thee down that the rain stop thee not. And it came to pass in the mean while, that the heaven was black with clouds and wind, and there was a great rain...* (1 Kings 18:42-45).

One of Jesus's parables stressed our power in continued intercession, not giving up but persevering in prayer:

> *And he spake a parable unto them to this end, that men ought always to pray, and not to faint; saying, There was in a city a judge, which feared not God, neither regarded man: and there was a widow in that city; and she came unto him, saying, Avenge me of mine adversary. And he would not for a while: but afterward he said within himself, Though I fear not God, nor regard man; yet because this widow troubleth me, I will avenge her; lest by her continual coming she weary me. And the Lord said, Hear what the unjust judge saith. And shall not God avenge his own elect, which cry day and night unto him though he bear long with them? I tell you that he will avenge them speedily...* (Luke 18:1-8).

Victory through prayer that goes beyond mere surface "wishing" is the guarantee of Jesus Himself:

> *Ask, and it shall be given you; seek, and ye shall find; knock, and it shall be opened unto you: for every one that asketh receiveth; and he that seeketh findeth; and to him that knocketh it shall be opened* (Matthew 7:7-8).

We ask on behalf of those in need, but it must not be left there. We must seek on their behalf, and knock, until we see the victory opened up completely. This is the promise upon which we can surely stand—a sure word from God Himself, one of the most tremendous weapons of warfare we can ever know. And it is in our hands. More than that, it is in our mouths.

## DISCUSSION QUESTIONS

1. In the past, have you been playing offense or defense for the Lord?
2. How different would your life look if you lived like you were at war, and there was no defense?

3. Do you think you could ever be a great intercessor like Moses?
4. How did Moses get to the point where he could intercede before God for the nation of Israel?
5. What steps can you take today to begin living a life of unceasing prayer and intercession?

## NOTE

1. See Morris Cerullo's book, *Proof Producers*, chapter entitled, "The Roots of the Battle."

Chapter 23

# WEAPONS OF OFFENSIVE WARFARE, PART 2: SPEAK THE WORD

The Word of God. There is no way to stress strongly enough the power of God's Word as both a defensive and an offensive weapon. We saw as we studied the temptations of Jesus how the written Word of God was used to thwart Satan's temptations and thus was a defensive weapon. However, it is one of the most powerful offensive weapons, if not the most powerful, that God has placed in our hands—more than that, in our mouths.

Conversely, our own words often are the most destructive force Satan uses against us. We have already seen that God's Word is the *"sword of the spirit"* (Ephesians 6:17). Now God Himself tells us what a powerful sword this weapon is in Hebrews, where it is written:

> *For the Word of God is quick, and powerful, and sharper than any twoedged sword, piercing even to the dividing asunder of soul and spirit, and of the joints and marrow, and is a discerner of the thoughts and intents of the heart* (Hebrews 4:12).

The sure, sharp sword is used for other purposes also, but our concern in this study is the weaponry of the Spirit. In a later chapter, we take up the power of God's Spirit and the utter necessity of this power to properly handle armor and weapons. In this chapter, however, we presuppose that you, as a child of God, use this potent sword, God's Word, by the Spirit. Anything less is lethal to spiritual life. *"...The letter killeth, but the spirit giveth life"* (2 Corinthians 3:6).

## USING THE SWORD

Sometimes, people use God's Word on others with the deadly intent of smiting, even killing that person spiritually, not of helping them or of showing compassion. Many, many people have been encouraged along the road to hell with God's Word carelessly or ignorantly used, twisted, or taken out of context. We, as God's elect, must not come from that position.

As soldiers in the Army of God, we must come from God's position, a position of the Spirit that is diametrically opposed to Satan in all his ways and forms. Jesus said: *"...the words that I speak unto you, they are spirit, and they are life"* (John 6:63). The Bible speaks of those who heard the Word of God and it profited them nothing because it was not mixed with faith.

> *For unto us was the gospel preached, as well as unto them: but the word preached did not profit them, not being mixed with faith in them that heard it* (Hebrews 4:2).

We also do not come from that position. We come from a position of faith because we know that God's Word is true. We can stand upon it and stake our lives upon it no matter what anyone or anything else says. *"...Let God be true, but every man a liar..."* (Romans 3:4).

God's Word is so powerful that it is the instrument of His very creativity. God actually created the worlds by the power of His Word—not by combustion, not by nuclear fission, not by some mystical or scientific process, but by His Word. The Bible says that Jehovah God stepped out on the precipice of space:

> *And God said, Let there be light: and there was light. ... And God said, Let there be a firmament in the midst of the waters...and it was so* (Genesis 1:3,6,7).

*"And God said...and God said...and God said"*—as God said, so it happened. As God said so, the fish began to swim, the mountains were carved out, the waters were separated from the earth, the stars were thrown into their orbits, the sun and the moon began to shine. *And God said...!* When God said it, it was so.

Think about the power of this Word that said, *"let there be life,"* and there was life. Life, substance, fowl, animals, stars, sun, moon coming into existence out of nothing, but by the Word of a voice. God's power was *in His Word.* What a weapon!

I pray that in the spirit you will receive the spiritual bombshell I am about to share with you. It is this: *God's Word is true when He speaks it, and it is true when we speak it.* God's Word not only is the written Word, but we may speak His Word—and it is an instrument, a weapon, and a strength to us.

Imagine for a moment the power of God's words in our mouths. *"I will make my words in thy mouth fire..."* (Jeremiah 5:14). If God could only help us to understand that the life and the power of His words are eternal. They do not have anything to do with the weakness of these human vessels that we are. Consider this powerful truth:

> *...For he hath said, I will never leave thee, nor forsake thee. So that we may boldly say, The Lord is my helper, and I will not fear what man shall do unto me* (Hebrews 13:5-6).

He hath said, so that we may boldly say! The writer is speaking about Jesus Christ: *"For he hath said, I will never leave thee, nor forsake thee."* I wish that the writer had not put the period there, and I wish he had not made a new verse out of the next verse:

> *For he hath said, I will never leave thee, nor forsake thee: so that we may boldly say, The Lord is my helper, and I will not fear what man shall do unto me.*

*He hath said...so that we may boldly say.* You can take this statement and put it in anything that God has ever said. What was true in God's mouth does not lose its trueness. It is just as true when you speak it as when God spoke it, because it is God's Word and God never lies. It is truth!

Therefore, God's Word is true in our mouths, and we still are living in defeat or merely "holding the fort," not operating in spiritually creative areas. We must be saying the wrong things, or the right words have not entered into our spirit. We must be using words that are not God's, words that are not power, words that are not truth, words that are not positive, words that are not creative, or we are not believing the words that are all of those things.

Here is one of the greatest truths in this book: Many times we say, or confess, things that bring our own defeat. Instead of being weapons against Satan, we turn our words upon ourselves. Our own words become Satan's weapons against us. *"Thou art snared with the words of thy mouth..."* (Proverbs 6:2).

## CONFESS VICTORY!

We have just finished a powerful chapter on the use of prayer as a weapon against Satan, but do you know that by praying wrong words we defeat ourselves? We say that we believe God's Word, but we speak the opposite, and by so doing, reveal that we do not really have God's faith. Jesus said:

> *Therefore I say unto you, what things soever ye desire, when ye pray, believe that ye receive them, and ye shall have them* (Mark 11:24).

Yet when we pray, we often say the very opposite. When we discuss our problems with others, we often say the opposite. Since God's Word is truth, the opposite word is a lie. Since God's Word is positive, the opposite word is negative. Since God's Word is creative, the opposite word is destructive. Since God's Word is light, the opposite word is darkness. Do you see it?

We tell our friends, "Well, I prayed and prayed, and things just got worse." That is not letting Mark 11:24 be His Word in our mouths. It is just the opposite. We can stand upon God's Word when we pray. We can utilize tremendous Scriptures. We can say, "God, You said..." and add His promises.

God, You said:

> *...If two or you shall agree on earth as touching any thing that they ask, it shall be done for them of my Father which is in heaven* (Matthew 18:19).

God, You said:

> *...No good thing will He withhold from them that walk uprightly* (Psalms 84:11).

You can say any of the thousands of promises that are ours in Christ Jesus and use them as a point of prayer for powerful prayer victories as outlined in the previous chapter. But God's Word is more than a power in prayer. It is a power just when we speak it out, when we confess it.

> *But what saith it? The word is night thee, even in thy mouth, and in thy heart: that is, the word of faith, which we preach; that if thou shalt confess with thy mouth...* (Romans 10:8-9).

Where is God's Word?

"In thy mouth!"

What must we do with it?

"Confess!"

What do we confess? Our feelings? Feelings lie. Satan can affect our feelings. Circumstances can affect our feelings. Our diet or lack of sleep can affect our feelings. Our feelings change. They are not a weapon. They are unreliable and useless in warfare. Feelings are carnal and we are told expressly that the weapons of our warfare are not carnal. That is why God says, *"...Let the weak say, I am strong"* (Joel 3:10).

Someone asks, "Brother Cerullo, if I am weak and I say that I am strong, won't I be lying?"

I would not be lying. God's Word says that I am strong and I know God's Word to be true. I know feelings can lie, but God's Word never can. If there is a difference between what I see, feel, hear, etc., and what I know to be God's Word, than seeing, feeling, and hearing lies. God's Word is still true. I am operating on the sixth sense that God has given me as His child—the supernatural sense called faith.[1]

God has said, *"With his stripes we are healed"* (Isaiah 53:5). When I am sick, this Word is health in my mouth: "Lord, I confess that with His stripes I am healed."

When you are going through some tremendous trial (and Christians often do), you can sit down and cry, or you can rise up in the power of God's Word and overcome. You can say, "God, by these tears, by my despondency, by my drooping spirit, what I am trying to say is that You are not meeting my need!" You would be denying the Word of God that says, *"My God shall supply all your need according to his riches in glory by Christ Jesus"* (Philippians 4:19). By that denial, you bring your own defeat—you are getting what you believe in!

Or in your trial you can say, "God, I confess that despite every circumstance I can see, You are meeting my need right now. I confess that You will never leave me or forsake me. I confess that 'My God shall supply all my needs in Christ Jesus.' I confess that 'I am more than a conqueror through Him who loved me.'"

Confess any Word of God. His Word is true. What He said is exactly what is going on—you are having your need met right now. You are not being left or forsaken by God. You are more than a conqueror through Him.

This chapter could go on and on. It could embrace every promise in the Word of God. However, a book like that already has been written. It is called the Holy Bible. What promises for spiritual victory it contains!

I will list just a few for you, but these are just the tip of the iceberg. Read, study, absorb the Word of God. Make every word your own. It will be a creative, victorious force in your mouth as you speak out and confess God's Word. Satan must flee in the face of this effective sword wielded by the power of God.

## PROMISES

God hath said:

> *...Whatsoever ye shall bind on earth shall be bound in heaven: and whatsoever ye shall loose on earth shall be loosed in heaven* (Mathew 18:18).

So that we may boldly say:

> *...Come out of the man, thou unclean spirit* (Mark 5:8).

God hath said:

> *...My peace I give unto you...* (John 14:27).

So that we may boldly say:

> *For God hath not given us the spirit of fear, but of power, and of love, and of a sound mind* (2 Timothy 1:7).

God hath said:

> *...No good thing will he withhold from them that walk uprightly* (Psalms 84:11).

So that we may boldly say:

> *The Lord will give strength unto his people...* (Psalms 29:11).

God hath said:

> *...I will never leave thee, nor forsake thee* (Hebrews 13:5).

So that we may boldly say:

*The eternal God is thy refuge, and underneath are the everlasting arms: and he shall thrust out the enemy from before thee; and shall say, Destroy them* (Deuteronomy 33:27).

God hath said:

*Fear thou not; for I am with thee…* (Isaiah 41:10).

So that we may boldly say:

*…The people that do know their God shall be strong, and do exploits* (Daniel 11:32).

God hath said:

*…With God all things are possible* (Matthew 19:26).

So that we may boldly say:

*…If thou canst believe, all things are possible to him that believeth* (Mark 9:23).

God hath said:

*The earth is the Lord's, and the fullness thereof…* (Psalms 24:1).

So that we may boldly say:

*…My God shall supply all* [my] *need according to his riches in glory by Christ Jesus* (Philippians 4:19).

God hath said:

*The Lord is my shepherd…* (Psalms 23:1).

So that we may boldly say:

*…I will fear no evil…* (Psalms 23:4).

God hath said:

*Fear thou not; for I am with thee…* (Isaiah 41:10).

So that we may boldly say:

…[He] *will uphold* [me] *with the right hand of* [His] *righteousness* (Isaiah 41:10).

God hath said:

> *...He preserveth the souls of his saints; he delivereth them out of the hand of the wicked* (Psalms 97:10).

So that we may boldly say:

> *In all these things we are more than conquerors through him that loved us* (Romans 8:37).

God hath said:

> *...Be strong in the Lord, and in the power of his might* (Ephesians 6:10).

So that we may boldly say:

> *...Taking the shield of faith, wherewith* [I] *shall be able to quench all the fiery darts of the wicked* (Ephesians 6:16).

## Discussion Questions

1. Have you ever allowed your words to confess defeat instead of victory and power in Christ?
2. Have Christians ever misused the Sword of the Spirit on you or someone you know, condemning and tearing you down rather than building you up with God's promises?
3. Which of the promises of God in this chapter are the most meaningful to you? Begin to recite them to yourself today, along with the verse that claims each promise for your own life.

### Note

1. See Morris Cerullo's book, *Why do the Righteous Suffer?* (Morris Cerullo World Evangelism, 1978).

CHAPTER 24

# WEAPONS OF OFFENSIVE WARFARE, PART 3: BINDING AND LOOSING

WHEN JESUS WAS WALKING IN the flesh here on earth, He was the walking example for the disciples who were to carry on His work after His death, resurrection, and ascension. This includes His use of the words of His mouth. We mentioned previously that although Jesus is God, while on earth He did not call upon His inherent deity. He also was 100 percent man. He utilized only those spiritual weapons and resources which also are available to us.

Jesus declared: "*...All power is given unto me in heaven and in earth*" (Matthew 28:18). He also said: *"Behold, I give unto you power...over all the power of the enemy"* (Luke 10:19). He further said: "*...as my Father hath sent me, even so send I you*" (John 20:21).

Here is the purpose for which God sent Jesus to this world:

> *...For this purpose the Son of God was manifested, that he might destroy the works of the devil* (1 John 3:8).

This is the same purpose for which we are sent. We are to destroy the works of the enemy. We do it by the same methods Jesus used.

## SPEAK THE WORD

Jesus was a master at the use of God's Word. The Scriptures give us clear teaching on methods of praying for the sick. However, as we enter into the authority delegated to us by Jesus Christ, we enter into a dimension even beyond that, a dimension in which Jesus Himself functioned to fulfill His God-given purpose. Though Jesus healed many sick and afflicted people and those who were demon possessed, we do not have a single record that Jesus ever once prayed for the sick.[1] He spoke the Word.

When the centurion came to Jesus on behalf of his servant who was paralyzed, he told Jesus, "You don't have to come to my house. Speak the word only and my servant will be healed." Jesus said:

> *...Go thy way; and as thou hast believed, so be it done unto thee. And his servant was healed in the selfsame hour* (Matthew 8:13).

The centurion had perceived something about Jesus which made him a man of great faith. We also will be people of great faith when we perceive this truth: He saw that Jesus Christ was a man under authority of God.

As an army officer, the centurion knew his soldiers would obey his slightest orders. With the eye of faith, he saw that Jesus had much greater authority, that He had authority over all things, and that His every word must be obeyed. Jesus had only to speak the word.

One day Jesus met a man in the synagogue who had a withered hand. Jesus did not pray for him to be healed. Instead He told the man, *"Stretch forth thine hand."* He spoke the word. In obedience the withered hand was completely healed (Mark 3:1-5).

A leper came to Jesus and declared, "Jesus, if You will, You can make me clean." Jesus did not pray for him. He said, *"I will; be thou clean."* He spoke the word; the leprosy disappeared (Matthew 8:2-3).

He said to the lame man at the pool, "Rise," and the man arose (see John 5:8). He said to the blind, "See," and the blind received their sight (see Luke 7:21). He said to the deaf, "Hear," and the deaf heard (see Mark 7:32-35). He said to the demons, "Come out," and they obeyed His word (see Matthew 9:32-33).

The religious leaders said:

> *...What thing is this? what new doctrine is this? for with authority commandeth he even the unclean spirits, and they do obey him* (Mark 1:27).

Jesus spoke the word to the winds and the waves, *"Peace, be still,"* and the storms subsided (Mark 4:39).

When Jesus came to Bethany where His friend Lazarus had died and had been buried for four days, Jesus did pray. However, His prayer was expressly for the purpose of letting those around Him know that His power was from God. He said:

> *...Father, I thank thee that thou hast heard me. And I knew that thou hearest me always: but because of the people which stand by I said it, that they may believe that thou hast sent me* (John 11:41-42).

When He wrought the deliverance, however, He did not say, "Now God, You bring Lazarus forth." He spoke directly to the corpse and commanded: "Lazarus, come forth."

> *And he that was dead came forth, bound hand and foot with graveclothes: and his face was bound about with a napkin. Jesus saith unto them, Loose him, and let him go* (John 11:44).

We not only see as the centurion did that Jesus had the authority to speak the Word, as His chosen disciples we see that we have been delegated His authority. If He could speak the Word and the work was done—and He gave us the same authority—we can speak the Word and see the work done. Jesus said:

> *...As my Father hath sent me, even so send I you* (John 20:21).

> *...Whosoever shall say unto this mountain, Be thou removed, and be thou cast into the sea; and shall no doubt in his heart,*

> *but shall believe all those things which he saith, shall come to pass; he shall have whatsoever he sayeth* (Mark 11:23).

We are now moving into an area that is based on prayer, yet is not prayer in the strict sense of the word. It is based on the Word of God. It is a new dimension of spiritual power that is never reached by many people. It is a dimension of speaking, with God's authority, words that God puts in our mouths so that no force of Satan dare stand before us. It is a dimension of power open to us, but never entered into by an overwhelming majority of God's people. It is one of the most powerful weapons in the Bible for spiritual warfare, and its scriptural foundation is found in this statement by Jesus:

> *...Whatsoever ye shall bind on earth shall be bound in heaven: and whatsoever ye shall loose on earth shall be loosed in heaven* (Matthew 18:18).

## Authority to Bind and Loose

This power of binding and loosing warrants a chapter by itself because it is not really prayer, and it is not solely the written Word of God. It is based on prayer by nature of the fact that in order to lay hold on this powerful weapon we must penetrate to a deeper dimension in prayer than most people ever dream about. We must learn to travail and prevail in prayer until we penetrate the spirit world to where we can exercise this authority God has given us to bind and to loose.

We cannot deal on a surface level with the spiritual battle that rages at the roots of every problem. The warfare is not on the surface. It is not in the circumstances as we see them. In order to fight the war, we have to get on the territory where that battle is taking place, and this is in the spirit world.

The weapon of binding and loosing is so powerful that we must be powerful, spiritual men and women to be able to use it. When David was fleeing from Saul, he sought Ahimelech, the priest, and asked him for a sword.

> *And the priest said, The sword of Goliath the Philistine whom thou slewest in the valley of Elah, behold, it is here wrapped in a cloth behind the ephod: if thou wilt take that, take it: for there is no other save that here...* (1 Samuel 21:9).

Goliath's sword was made for a giant. An ordinary person could not use it. However, David had grown and matured in warfare from the time he had been unable to maneuver in Saul's armor (see 1 Samuel 17:38-39). He now had experience in warfare and confidence in his authority. He rose up in faith to handle this larger weapon than he had heretofore used and he boldly declared: "*...There is none like that; give it me*" (1 Samuel 21:9)

The ability to bind may be larger, more powerful weaponry than some of us have ever used. In the authority of God's Word, let us rise up in faith and say of this weapon God has given us: "Give it me. There is none like it." This is the sword of spiritual giants. We can be those giants.

Ready for prevailing spiritual battle, we have come to the place where one of the gifts of God's Holy Spirit is an absolute essential must to the spiritual warrior, and that is the discerning of spirits (see 1 Corinthians 12:10). How can we fight what we do not see or discern? How can we fight if we do not know what the enemy is? We know that overall it is Satan and we certainly can come against him and all his power, but we have added leverage if we can call out the spirits by name as we bind them.

One reason that some people are so ineffective in this area is that they do not discern the real issues at stake. We are not in the arena in the power of God, clothed with His armor, bearing His weapons, recognizing and discerning the enemy. We are prepared to let God's Word be our two-edged sword of the Spirit.

## The Sword

There are several explanations of the two edges. One truth is this: We have the written Word of God which we know is true and upon which we can stand at any time and in any circumstance.

God also gives us the spoken word, spoken by His power in the same manner Jesus used. God can and does put inspired words in the mouths of His ministers as they move under the unction and anointing of His Holy Spirit.

When I was in India at the time the revelation of the New Anointing was given to me (as I related previously), as I entered into the spirit world in prayer, I began to call out and bind such spirits as were there to hinder our crusade in that country. I bound the spirits of sin, the spirit of false idols, the false cults, the spirit of false religion, every devilish spirit I knew was at work there against us. I found myself binding the power of Satan which controlled the religious leaders and might influence them to try to destroy the crusade. In Jesus's Name I bound them and I cast them out. Then I began to loose the spirits which would bless the crusade efforts.

This has been a stumbling block to some immature Christians—that there are many good spirits. They quoted the verse that says: *"For by one Spirit are we all baptized into one body..."* (1 Corinthians 12:13). It is true that there is one Holy Spirit, which is the Spirit of God, but remember that all truth is parallel. As there are many evil spirits emanating from Satan, there are also good spirits which emanate from the Lord.

The spirits of rebellion, confusion, frustration, turmoil, lust, promiscuousness, sin, drugs, unconcern, selfishness, criticism, fear, and anxiety are all loose in the world. Some of our modern-day Christians are so confused that they do not know the will of God. They do not know where to go; they do not know what to do; they do not know where to turn. They just do not know what decision to make. They operate in a spirit of frustration and uncertainty. Contrast that with the spirit of steadfastness known by the apostle Paul who said:

> *...I know whom I have believed, and am persuaded that he is able to keep that which I have committed unto him against that day* (2 Timothy 1:12).

> *Who shall separate us from the love of Christ? shall tribulation, or distress, or persecution, or famine, or nakedness, or*

> *peril, or sword? ...Nay, in all these things we are more than conquerors through him that loved us* (Romans 8:35,37).

As evil is a spirit, good is a spirit. As hate is a spirit which has infiltrated and ruled this nation and the world, so love is a spirit. As frustration and confusion are spirits, so is steadfastness. Sickness is a spirit. It is a result of the curse. God never intended for man's eyes to become dim or his ears to become weak or even for him to lose his hair.

Healing also is a spirit. Many ministers have been amazed that all of a sudden people would begin to get healed in their services. No matter what they preached on, people all over the congregation would start receiving their healings. Then suddenly it would stop. What happened was that a spirit of healing was present in the meetings.

That is why I emphasize over and over in my meetings that I do not need to touch a person for them to be healed. "God is a Spirit. He is right there beside you," I tell the congregation. All over the auditorium people will begin to have miraculous healings as the spirit of healing moves through the room. A pastor might notice souls being saved in every service, no matter what kind of service it is. When this happens, a spirit of salvation is moving in the service.

People have different spirits operating in and influencing them, and often these spirits are contagious. Perhaps someone will come in with a spirit of confusion. Before you know it, that spirit has spread. Or it may be a spirit of contention or a spirit of lust. People walk in their own spiritual atmosphere, and their spirits affect the spirits of others. One person with a spirit of contention can affect a whole building of co-workers. Conversely, one person with a spirit of enthusiasm or friendliness can affect that same building for good.

Some atmospheres are so heavy with bad spirits—unforgiveness, selfishness, discouragement, hatred, prejudice, etc.—that you can feel it. Some are so full of good spirits such as friendliness, love, openness, etc., that you receive a lift just by entering the room. You cannot fight a spirit of contention with contentiousness in your own spirit. That just adds confusion to confusion. You fight evil spirits by binding them and their power and by loosing good spirits in their place.

This is something that is done here on earth. You may be on your knees in the I Care Prayer Center, in your dormitory room, in the park, or some other earthly setting, but if you are binding or loosing spirits, you are operating in a spiritual realm. What you do on earth is done in heaven. In the Spirit of God you utter the words here on earth, and those words are carried out in the spirit world.

God's earth is a great arena of spiritual warfare, and this is where the major battles must be fought and won. If your family relationships are tangled, in the spirit you can bind that foul spirit of contention or rebellion and cast it out. You can loose a spirit of forgiveness, a spirit of love.

If you have met God's conditions of giving and are still having financial problems, and if it appears that all your resources are going down the drain no matter what you do, you can bind the spirit of poverty and loose the spirit of abundance on your means. You can bind a spirit of confusion and loose a spirit of peace and well-being. In the Name of Jesus Christ and by the power of God's Holy Spirit you can bind any evil spirit and loose God's goodness into any situation as long as you are doing it in the arena of spiritual warfare.

There is no need to let perplexities and problems run rampant through our lives or those of our loved ones. We have the authority and the dominion to stop it now and see a complete turnabout in the situation. Every battle is spiritual in scope, and we have the weapons to win if we will just rise up and do it.

## Discussion Questions

1. Is there a situation where you have been praying for God's help but have not seen an answer?
2. What does the Word of God say about your situation? Begin to speak His Word over it.

3. What evil spirits might be working in this situation? Begin to act on your authority to bind evil and loose blessing!

## Note

1. See Chapter 13 of Morris Cerullo's book *Proof Producers* entitled, "The Methodology of Producing the Proof."

CHAPTER 25

# WEAPONS OF OFFENSIVE WARFARE, PART 4: FASTING AND FAITH

WE COME NOW TO A subject that is at the same time a tremendous battle, and yet one of the most forceful weapons for fighting spiritual battles that we have at our command—fasting. Fasting often is spoken of in conjunction with prayer, and the two do go hand in glove. However, Jesus mentions each as an individual act:

> *And when thou prayest, thou shall not be as the hypocrites are: for they love to pray standing in the synagogues and in the corners of the streets, that they may be seen of men.... Moreover when ye fast, be not, as the hypocrites, of a sad countenance: for they disfigure their faces, that they may appear unto men to fast...* (Matthew 6:5,16).

## THE REMEDY FOR UNBELIEF

As we stressed earlier, many weapons overlap and interface. As we do well to use the whole armor of God in our defense, it is equally important to use the entire arsenal of God's weapons for the offensive tearing down of Satan's strongholds. Jesus's disciples were commissioned to go out to preach the Gospel, heal the sick, and cast out devils. They did this with such success that they returned rejoicing that *"even the devils are subject unto us"* (Luke 10:17).

Despite the commission Jesus gave them and the delegation of His authority to carry out the commission, and despite successful ministry in the past, there came a time when the disciples found themselves powerless to cast out a demon. The account of this is given in Matthew 17:14-21 and also in Mark 9:14-29. This incident took place as Jesus was returning from the Mount of Transfiguration with Peter, James, and John. There was a great tumult among the multitude awaiting Him. At His inquiry, one of the men ran to explain what the problem was:

> *And when he came to his disciples, he saw a great multitude about them, and the scribes questioning with them. And straightway all the people, when they beheld him, were greatly amazed, and running to him saluted him. And he asked the scribes, What question ye with them? And one of the multitude answered and said, Master, I have brought unto thee my son which hath a dumb spirit; and wheresoever he taketh him, he teareth him: and he foameth, and gnasheth with his teeth, and pineth away: and I spake to thy disciples that they should cast him out; and they could not* (Mark 9:14-18).

Though the disciples were unable to cope with the need, Jesus was not. The results of His ministry are told in verses 25-27:

> *When Jesus saw that the people came running together, he rebuked the foul spirit, saying unto him, Thou dumb and deaf spirit, I charge thee, come out of him, and enter no more into him. And the spirit cried, and rent him sore, and came out of him: and he was as one dead; insomuch that many said, He is dead. But Jesus took him by the hand, and lifted him up; and he arose* (Mark 9:25-27).

Before Jesus rebuked the devil, however, He rebuked those around as a faithless and perverse generation.

> *Then Jesus answered and said, O faithless and perverse generation, how long shall I be with you? how long shall I suffer you? bring him hither to me* (Matthew 17:17).

When the disciples asked Jesus why they had been unable to cast the demon out, He told them it was because of their unbelief (see Matthew 17:20).

Since Jesus told the disciples that they could not cast the demon out because of their unbelief and then declared that this kind came out only by prayer and fasting, it is obvious that prayer and fasting was the remedy for the unbelief. Prayer and fasting would have given them that added impetus and power needed to meet the need.

If such a demon could be cast out only by prayer and fasting and yet Jesus immediately did it, it is equally obvious that He already had prayed and fasted. The Scriptures report of Jesus's prayer life time and again that He often spent time with God.

> *And in the morning, rising up a great while before day, he went out, and departed into a solitary place, and there prayed* (Mark 1:35).

> *And when he had sent the multitudes away, he went up into a mountain apart to pray: and when the evening was come, he was there alone* (Matthew 14:23).

When Lazarus died and was buried for four days, Jesus spoke the word of power that brought Lazarus forth from the grave, but it was obvious that Jesus had been in prayer long before the need for ministry arose. Before He called Lazarus forth, Jesus turned His eyes heavenward and said: "*...Father, I thank thee that thou hast heard me*" (John 11:41). Notice the past tense. The preparation for ministry had already been made. When the need arose, the work could be accomplished on the spot.

The pull of the world is continually downward. As a Christian ministers the things of the Lord, he must be careful to tarry before

God to replenish his spiritual supply for coming needs. This preparation must include not only prayer, but fasting as well, for there are some things that can be accomplished through no other means.

That fasting can be of great physical benefit to the body is generally recognized throughout the world today as a means of cleansing and purifying the system. Of far greater benefit to the Christian, however, is the spiritual strength provided through scriptural fasting. It is of such benefit as a spiritual weapon that Satan fights very hard to prevent true fasting.

Our spiritual battles often involve our physical senses and needs, and fasting is no exception. To fast unto God as a spiritual exercise is one of the hardest exercises of godliness that is known, for to do so is to deny one of the fundamental appetites of the flesh. Galatians 5:17 tells us that:

> *The flesh lusteth against the spirit, and the Spirit against the flesh: and these are contrary the one to the other: so that ye cannot do the things that ye would.*

Matthew 26:41 tells us that, *"the spirit indeed is willing, but the flesh is weak."* Still another verse, Romans 8:7, tells us that the carnal or fleshly mind is *"enmity against God."* The pull of the world and of the flesh is constantly a downward pull. The pull of the Spirit in Christ Jesus is up, a lifting into the heavenlies, a strengthening of might in the *"inner man"* (Ephesians 3:16).

It is through fasting that we have the most effective means for loosing the transcendency of the flesh and bringing the body under submission so that we may operate and minister in spiritual realms.

## Types of Fasts

There are several kinds of fasting, different lengths of fasts, and several reasons for fasting detailed in the Bible. There is a fast from God which permits drinking of water; there is a complete fast which includes abstinence from water; and there is a partial fast which, in effect, is a restricted diet. There are private fasts which are between the seeker and God alone, and there are public fasts which are called by religious or governmental leaders. All of these are honored by God when scripturally applied.

It seems clear from the scriptures that the fast of Jesus recorded in Matthew 4:2 and Luke 4:2 was a fast from food only. At the end of 40 days, Jesus was hungry but the Bible does not say that He was thirsty. Since the need for water is much greater than that of food, and since Satan tempted Jesus with something to eat, not with something to drink, it stands to reason that Jesus had water during this wilderness time.

Moses was on two nearly consecutive 40-day fasts with neither food nor water:

> *When I was gone up into the mount to receive the tables of stone, even the tables of the covenant which the Lord made with you, then I abode in the mount forty days and forty nights, I neither did eat bread nor drink water* (Deuteronomy 9:9).

He was supernaturally sustained by God, because going for more than three or four days without water normally harms the body.

There are several fasts without water listed in the Bible. Ezra did it:

> *Then Ezra rose up from before the house of God, and went into the chamber of Johanan the son of Eliashib: and when he came thither, he did eat no bread, nor drink water: for he mourned because of the transgression of them that had been carried away* (Ezra 10:6).

When Queen Esther made her valiant plea for the salvation of the Jews before King Ahaseurus, she requested Mordecai to call a fast of the Jews in Shushan. This is one instance in which prayer is not mentioned in connection with the fast, though it must be assumed that the people already were praying for deliverance.

> *Go, gather together all the Jews that are present in Shushan, and fast ye for me, and neither eat nor drink three days, night or day: I also and my maidens will fast likewise; and so will*

> *I go in unto the king, which is not according to the law: and if I perish, I perish* (Esther 4:16).

Immediately upon Paul's conversion, he went on a three-day abstinence from food and water: *"And he was three days without sight, and neither did eat nor drink"* (Acts 9:9). Daniel was seeking God at the time of his great visitation as related in the tenth chapter of Daniel. He went on a partial fast, probably the barest necessities, for three weeks:

> *In those days I Daniel was mourning three full weeks. I ate no pleasant bread, neither came flesh nor wine in my mouth, neither did I anoint myself at all, till three whole weeks were fulfilled* (Daniel 10:2-3).

In another instance he says:

> *And I set my face unto the Lord God, to seek by prayer and supplications, with fasting, and sackcloth, and ashes* (Daniel 9:3).

These are all examples of individuals fasting before God. There were times, however, that battles were turned because of organized fasts called by leaders. Nineveh was spared from annihilation through a fast called by the head of the government:

> *And Jonah began to enter into the city a day's journey, and he cried, and said, Yet forty days, and Nineveh shall be overthrown. So the people of Nineveh believed God, and proclaimed a fast, and put on sackcloth, from the greatest of them even to the least of them. For word came unto the king of Nineveh, and he arose from his throne, and he laid his robe from him, and covered him with sackcloth, and sat in ashes. And he caused it to be proclaimed and published through Nineveh by the decree of the king and his nobles saying, Let neither man nor beast, herd nor flock, taste anything: let them not feed, nor drink water: but let man and beast be covered with sackcloth, and cry mightily unto God; yea, let them turn every one from his evil way, and from the*

> *violence that is in their hands. Who can tell if God will turn and repent, and turn away from his fierce anger, that we perish not? And God saw their works, that they turned from their evil way; and God repented of the evil, that he had said that he would do unto them; and he did it not* (Jonah 3:4-10).

The children of Israel won a great victory against overwhelming odds when King Jehoshaphat called a fast:

> *And Jehoshaphat feared, and set himself to seek the Lord, and proclaimed a fast throughout all Judah* (2 Chronicles 20:3).

When a spiritual authority calls a fast, those under that authority should never use the excuse, "I do not feel led to fast." They should exercise obedience, as group fasting has been mightily used even to the changing of God's mind (as in the case of Nineveh).

There are several dangers inherent in fasting that are not exercised under the control of God. One is that a regularly scheduled fast, such as every Friday, may get to be a form devoid of real meaning and power unless an attitude of worship is maintained. In that respect it could also become a matter of pride or self-righteousness.

The Pharisee prayed, *"I fast twice in the week..."* (Luke 18:12). The publican could not even lift up his head. He could only pray, *"God be merciful to me a sinner"* (Luke 18:13). However, he was the one who went to his home justified, not the man who fasted twice a week. That is why Jesus enjoined us not to pray to be seen of men (Matthew 6:5).

During the time of Isaiah, the people were fasting, and God turned a deaf ear. Isaiah had this to say:

> *Wherefore have we fasted, say they, and thou seest not? Wherefore have we afflicted our soul, and thou takest no knowledge? Behold, in the day of your fast ye find pleasure, and exact all your labours. Behold, ye fast for strife and debate, and to smite with the fist of wickedness: ye shall not fast as ye do this day, to make your voice to be heard on high. Is it such a fast*

*that I have chosen? a day for a man to afflict his soul? is it to bow down his head as a bulrush, and to spread sackcloth and ashes under him? wilt thou call this a fast, and an acceptable day to the Lord? Is not this the fast that I have chosen? to loose the bands of wickedness, to undo the heavy burdens, and to let the oppressed go free, and that ye break every yoke? Is it not to deal thy bread to the hungry, and that thou bring the poor that are cast out to thy house? When thou seest the naked, that thou cover him; and that thou hide not thyself from thine own flesh?* (Isaiah 58:3-7)

The fast that God chooses is the one that brings liberty to the captive and help to the needy. When this type of fasting is sincerely employed, the results are almost staggering. The Christian is strengthened with might in the inner man, capable of waging spiritual warfare with great power, with this kind of testimony behind it:

*Then shall thy light break forth as the morning, and thine health shall spring forth speedily: and thy righteousness shall go before thee; the glory of the Lord shall be thy reward. Then shalt thou call, and the Lord shall answer; thou shalt cry, and he shall say, Here I am. If thou take away from the midst of thee the yoke, the putting forth of the finger, and speaking vanity; and if thou draw out thy soul to the hungry, and satisfy the afflicted soul; then shall thy light rise in obscurity and thy darkness be as the noon day: and the Lord shall guide thee continually, and satisfy thy soul in drought, and make fat thy bones: and thou shalt be like a watered garden, and like a spring of water, whose waters fail not* (Isaiah 58:8-11).

When such a prepared vessel is brought into the arena of confrontation with Satan and all of his power, Satan will have to flee—a defeated foe.

## Discussion Questions

1. Are there areas in your life where you struggle with unbelief or where your faith feels weak?

2. Have you ever tried any of the types of fasts in the Bible?
3. If you have never fasted before and you need more of God in your life, ask Him where He would have you start, then re-read the types of fasts. Whatever He points out to you—do it!

## Chapter 26

# SPIRITUAL FIREPOWER

Much spiritual dynamite has been included in these chapters, enough for anyone who reads it and absorbs it to experience victory over Satan continually in every circumstance. It is all firepower that is available to anyone with a spiritual eye to see or a spiritual ear to hear. Why then are so few people exercising the power and authority God has given us over Satan?

Too long the devil has kept the level of our faith far below what God has for us. Satan has many people convinced that their condition is hopeless, that the condition of the world itself is hopeless. People have problems that they cannot solve, sicknesses for which they cannot receive healing. They are carrying heavy, heavy burdens. Likewise, nations seem overwhelmed with problems, perplexities, pitfalls.

People and nations are crying for the kind of weapons and strategy that we already know. The real purpose of this book is not just to know with our minds, however. It is to motivate men and women to reach out into the realms of the Spirit where victories are won. Faith is a fact, but faith is an act.

I tell you in the Name of Jesus Christ, you are going to receive the faith that you need to rise up and take the limits off God to meet the needs in your life and your ministry, to know that the God we serve is the God who knows no limit. It is He Who holds the power to take this world for Him, power He wants to delegate to us.

## Remove the Limits on God!

Many people believe that God wants to be a mystery, that He wants to cloud Himself and hide Himself. They think that God takes great pleasure in being eerie and mystical. The one who is eerie, and who clouds himself in mystery, is Satan and all of his works. God is very simple. He is so clear that you can see Him as looking into a mirror. He is no mystery. He wants you to know the height, the length, the width, the breadth of His love and to understand all about Him.

> *That Christ may dwell in your hearts by faith; that ye, being rooted and grounded in love, may be able to comprehend with all saints what is the breadth, and length, and depth, and height; and to know the love of Christ, which passeth knowledge, that ye might be filled with all the fulness of God* (Ephesians 3:17-19).

Until the Church of Jesus Christ is filled with all the fullness of God, we will never take the world for God.

In 1978, God spoke to me and told me, "Son, I am going to use you to lead My people in how to take the limits off God." Then God said, "They in turn will be used by Me to reach the world."

There are many reasons why the Church of Jesus Christ limits an unlimited God. Unless you deal with them, they will relegate your life to conventional Christianity. We must get out of the ruts of the harvest and climb some spiritual ladders until we get into that place with God, where God can use us in the same way that He used the early Church. Lives must be changed. Minds must be changed. Spirits must be changed. Attitudes must be changed.

I am not talking about mind power or the power of positive thinking. I am not talking about any natural power at all. What I am talking about is the power that works inside you, the fullness of God, the firepower of the Spirit which causes us to rise up and march in victory over Satan. One of the great reasons why we limit God and go through the same spiritual routines and ruts in our lives over and over is because we do not go far enough.

Most in Christian experience go only to a certain point. They jerk, shake, dance, jiggle, and get goose bumps, but that is about all. They come to the point of blessing, they have a lot of feeling, but let them go out onto the street where somebody rubs them the wrong way and watch how long that blessing lasts. Watch how shallow the experience is to carry them through the times and the places where they need to manifest the fullness of God inside of them.

Until the Church of Jesus Christ goes past this point, there is no hope for the world—no hope! Until you are willing to lose every feeling you have—until you are willing to die instead of trying to assert yourself, trying to put that "I" and that self forth—until that happens, we will never take this world for Jesus Christ. It is not enough to sing it. It is not enough to preach it. Something has got to happen to us where it becomes an experience in our lives. Whenever we go out in mind power, in the spirit of self, we struggle. We struggle spiritually to reach up to try to get the things that we think God has for us—His promises and His blessings.

## THE EXPERIENCE—POWER!

Two thousand years ago, the Church was born with a peculiar ingredient. It was not born weak; it was not born anemic; it was not born spiritless; it was born with a very peculiar ingredient. The Church was not born through just the 12 apostles. There were 120 people in the upper room on the day of Pentecost. We limit God to 12 apostles and we think that everything was built and established upon them. It is true that God set the apostles in the Church, but every individual in the Church who was a follower of Jesus Christ was a minister of a unique characteristic.

When Jesus ascended, He gave His disciples a commission to, *"Go ye into all the world, and preach the Gospel to every creature"*

(Mark 16:15). "But," He said, "do not go yet. There is something you must do first; something you must wait for."

Jesus looked at these poor, uneducated fishermen He had called. He did not say to them, "Wait until you have had three years of Bible school. Don't go out until you get your theological degree from the seminary." He did not say, "Tarry here until you get goose bumps," or, "Wait until you are speaking in other tongues." He did not say any of those things. What He said was this: "I am going to give you an experience."

Our problem is that we have been going out without an experience. With all due respect to pastors, evangelists, ministers and missionaries, we can never save this world from behind the pulpit. God wants to raise up men, women, widows, farmers, lawyers, doctors, etc. He wants to take the grass roots. He wants to work with you in the sphere of your own activity and endue you with a special characteristic.

I do not think the devil minds people speaking in other tongues. Look at the lives of many of those who do—how many souls are they winning? How much are they really going out and working for the Lord Jesus Christ? How concerned are they about a lost world? I do not make light of speaking in tongues. I speak in tongues every day of my life. The prayer language of the Holy Spirit has a very distinct purpose in our lives.

I do not think the devil cares if you memorize the whole Bible. He does not mind your taking any kind of weapon at all—whether it is tongues or the Word—as long as you keep cleaning it, polishing it, and playing with it. *The only time the devil minds your taking a weapon is if you pick it up, load it, and use it for the purpose that God intended it to be used.*

When John the Baptist came, he cried, "Do not look at me. I am not the promised Messiah, but there is somebody coming after me who is mightier than I, whose shoes I am not even worthy to unloose. He is mightier than I and He will baptize you with the Holy Ghost and with fire" (see Matthew 3:11).

Jesus told His disciples they must go out to face this world and preach the Gospel, but He told them, "Do not dare leave Jerusalem until you are endued with power" (see Luke 24:49).

Power!

Power!

Power!

Suppose your life was represented by a glass half filled with water. The water could be like the Spirit. There are many people who are only half filled. Others are three quarters filled. A vessel can have various levels. Only God can judge how much an individual commits himself and what measure of the Spirit lies within that individual. An effective individual can and must be filled to the top.

Many people are filled with the Spirit who are not fully baptized. Many who speak in other tongues are not fully baptized in the Holy Ghost. With the great move of the Charismatics, we have set people down and said, "Say what I say." There comes a little jabbering, but not the power.

Many ministers declare that when Jesus said, *"Tarry ye in the city of Jerusalem, until ye be endued with power,"* it had a different meaning than it does now (Luke 24:49). They have come along with a new, modern, twentieth-century philosophy, trying to make instant spiritual giants. It cannot be done. They sit converts in chairs and say, "You don't need to tarry any longer, because that word 'tarry' means 'just receive.' All you have to do is sit there and instantly receive."

I am not against instantly receiving the prayer language of the Holy Spirit, but it took the followers of Jesus ten days, night and day in the Presence of God, waiting before God until they were endued with power. No one is going to be baptized in the Holy Spirit unless he learns the secret of waiting in the Presence of Almighty God. We must get down on our faces and be willing to spend all night praying, crying out, laying ourselves bare before Almighty God until He endues us with power from on high.

One day Peter saw a man lame since birth. He said:

> *Silver and gold have I none; but such as I have give I thee: in the Name of Jesus Christ of Nazareth rise up and walk* (Acts 3:6).

Then he took the lame man by the hand, lifted him to his feet, and the man was made whole. This was the same Peter who slept when Jesus prayed, the same Peter who denied Jesus. This was the same man who could not be found at the cross when Jesus hung there for the sins of the world. This was the same man who, when somebody said to him, "We have seen Jesus. He is alive. He is resurrected. He lives," this is the same man who said, "I don't believe it." Now he stood forth and exercised faith in the Name of Jesus, and a great miracle occurred.

Peter was exercising faith, but it was tied to an experience. He had been in the upper room. Cloven tongues of fire had fallen on him. He was baptized with the Holy Ghost. Now he walked down the street with the Holy Spirit in his life without measure. He was not speaking in other tongues like sounding brass and tinkling cymbals. He was now moving with the Sprit without measure. He was able to say, "I have been endued with power!"

The disciples did not just stand there in the upper room. They cried out to God. They laid themselves bare. They confessed their sins. They asked God for forgiveness where they had failed Him. They humbled themselves in the Presence of Almighty God until God endued them with power, until He baptized them with the Holy Ghost. Then and only then were they equipped with the good force that could win over the evil force. Then and only then were they filled with the power of God that is able to overthrow every power of Satan.

> *Ye are of God, little children, and have overcome them: because greater is he that is in you, than he that is in the world* (1 John 4:4).

> *Behold, I give unto you power to tread on serpents and scorpions, and over all the power of the enemy: and nothing shall by any means hurt you* (Luke 10:19).

There is no reason for living in defeat or seeing Satan triumph in battles around us when God has made us more than conquerors.

> *Nay, in all these things we are more than conquerors through him that loved us* (Romans 8:37).

## Claim the Victory!

We have the victory not just in the days to come, but we are—present tense—more than conquerors right now. God has provided everything we need to make us successful, not only in withstanding Satan, but actually penetrating his strongholds and tearing them down by the power of Christ.

> *For the weapons of our warfare are not carnal, but mighty through God to the pulling down of strong holds* (2 Corinthians 10:4).

We need never lose this battle; Jesus Himself will come and set up His rule, putting all enemies under His feet!

> *Then cometh the end, when he* [Jesus] *shall have delivered up the kingdom of God, even the Father; when he shall have put down all rule and all authority and power. For he must reign, till he hath put all enemies under his feet* (1 Corinthians 15:24-25).

The greatest activity of Satan on earth will take place during the tribulation period when he will particularly persecute the Jews. Revelation 12:7-17 tells of a war in the heavenlies between Michael and his angels and Satan and his angels. As a result, Satan is cast out of the heavenlies and the earth does become his main arena. Verse 12 points out that his wrath is increased because of the shortness of time that will then be left him. The woman he persecutes and with whom he makes war is Israel:

> *And there was war in heaven: Michael and his angels fought against the dragon; and the dragon fought and his angels, and prevailed not; neither was their place found any more in heaven. And the great dragon was cast out, that old serpent, called the Devil, and Satan, which deceiveth the whole world: he was cast out into the earth, and his angels were cast out with him. And I heard a loud voice saying in heaven, Now is come salvation, and strength, and the kingdom of our God, and the power of his Christ: for the accuser of our brethren is cast down, which accused them before our God day and night. And they overcame him by the blood of the Lamb, and by the word of their testimony; and they loved not their lives unto the death. Therefore rejoice, ye heavens, and ye that dwell in them. Woe to the inhabiters of the earth and of the sea! for the devil is come down unto you, having great wrath, because he knoweth that he hath but a short time. And when the dragon saw that he was cast unto the earth, he persecuted the woman which brought forth the man child. And to the woman were given two wings of a great eagle, that she might fly into the wilderness, into her place, where she is nourished for a time, and times, and half a time, from the face of the serpent. And the serpent cast out of his mouth water as a flood after the woman, that he might cause her to be carried away of the flood. And the earth helped the woman, and the earth opened her mouth, and swallowed up the flood which the dragon cast out of his mouth. And the dragon was wroth with the woman, and went to make war with the remnant of her seed, which keep the commandments of God, and have the testimony of Jesus Christ* (Revelation 12:7-17).

Satan gives the fullness of his power to the beast, or the Antichrist, for the duration of the tribulation period. This book does not purport to be a study of that period. However, any study of spiritual warfare needs to include the final outcome. Here are some of the activities that will culminate in Satan's final defeat:

1. Christ comes from heaven with His forces and defeats the forces of the Antichrist (see Revelation 19).
2. The beast and his false prophet are cast into the lake of fire (see Revelation 19:20).
3. The devil is cast into the bottomless pit for 1,000 years (known as the millennium) and is then loosed for "a little season."

> *And I saw an angel come down from heaven, having the key of the bottomless pit and a great chain in his hand. And he laid hold on the dragon, that old serpent, which is the Devil, and Satan, and bound him a thousand years, and cast him into the bottomless pit, and shut him up, and set a seal upon him, that he should deceive the nations no more, till the thousand years should be fulfilled: and after that he must be loosed a little season* (Revelation 20:1-3).

4. Satan is loosed and gathers the nations against Jerusalem. Fire from heaven destroys his armies (see Revelation 20:7-9).
5. Satan is vanquished once and for all.

> *And the devil that deceived them was cast into the lake of fire and brimstone, where the beast and the false prophet are, and shall be tormented day and night for ever and ever* (Revelation 20:10).

The picture of a laughing Satan reigning over souls in hell is just not scriptural. He himself will end in the lake of fire where hell also will be cast. Satan will know torment forever and ever. The prophecy of God pronounced upon him in Ezekiel and in Isaiah will have been fulfilled.

> *Thou hast defiled thy sanctuaries by the multitude of thine iniquities, by the iniquity of thy traffick; therefore will I bring forth a fire from the midst of thee, it shall devour thee, and I will bring thee to ashes upon the earth in the sight of*

> *all them that behold thee. All they that know thee among the people shall be astonished at thee: thou shalt be a terror, and never shalt thou be any more* (Ezekiel 28:18-19).
>
> *Yet thou shalt be brought down to hell, to the sides of the pit. They that see thee shall narrowly look upon thee, and consider thee, saying, Is this the man that made the earth to tremble, that did shake kingdoms; that made the world as a wilderness, and destroyed the cities thereof; that opened not the house of his prisoners?* (Isaiah 14:15-17)

This is the time when natural eyes will be able to see Satan's defeat. However—and this is what this book is all about—the spiritual eye can see Satan's defeat now and rise up in victory, for that defeat already has been accomplished by Jesus Christ. The cross of Calvary, meant by Satan to be the final victory for the forces of evil, was instead the very instrument of victory for Christ and all His followers.

I can see the devil having himself a great big field day when Jesus Christ was buried in the tomb. Down in that big, black, ugly abyss of the throne room of Satan all the demons of hell had been called to worship the devil because Jesus Christ, the Son of God, was dead. He had died on the cross. The devil sat back in his wicked glee and said, "I have conquered the Son of God." The devil did not know it, but on that first day, second day, and third day the blood of Jesus Christ was ascending to the throne of Jehovah God to make atonement for the sins of the world.

The pattern given to Moses and Aaron in the Old Testament was that the blood from the sacrificial lamb was to be caught in a basin. On the first Passover when Israel was delivered from the bondage of Egypt (which is in biblical language a type of sin), we see the blood of the sacrificial lamb being caught so that it would be applied to the lintel and the door post of each home (see Exodus 12:7). The sacrifice was not enough; the application of the blood had to take place, or death to the eldest son would have occurred as it did to the Egyptians. Moses commanded the Israelites:

*And ye shall take a bunch of hyssop, and dip it in the blood that is in the bason, and strike the lintel and the two side posts with the blood that is in the bason; and none of you shall go out at the door of his house until the morning* (Exodus 12:22).

So, the hands of Jehovah, so to speak, had reached down on that cross and caught the blood of Jesus. That blood was rising to the throne room of the Father, being presented as an everlasting, once and for all atonement for the sins of the world. The sacrifice has been accomplished, but now the application of that blood has to be made to the door of the human heart in order to cleanse it from sin and remove from it the specter of eternal death.

Those who would like to believe the fantasy that once you have had the blood applied to your heart, it does not matter what you do from then on because you are saved once and for all, should look at the fact that Moses told them that even after they had applied the blood to the door post they were not to leave the covering of that house or they would be subject to the same fate as the Egyptians. The Old Testament required that the blood be sprinkled upon the mercy seat.

*And he shall take of the blood of the bullock, and sprinkle it with his finger upon the mercy seat...* (Leviticus 16:14).

On the third day as this message reverberated from one end of God's creation to the other, something began to happen. A little light began to flicker in the throne room of hell where the great victory orgy was in full swing. That light began to get brighter and brighter until it filled the whole place where Satan and his demons were gathered. Those demons began to scream and cry out as they had never done before because they cannot stand light—their deeds are evil.

The devil came and bowed before that light. You say, "Brother Cerullo, there is no light in the throne room of the enemy." There was a light there this day! It was the light of the Son of God, because on the third day the devil could not hold Him, the grave could not keep Him, death could not swallow Him up. On the third day He arose, and He walked down into the throne room of the enemy.

It is written:

> *The Spirit of the Lord God is upon me...he hath sent me to bind up the brokenhearted, to proclaim liberty to the captives, and the opening of the prison to them that are bound* (Isaiah 61:1).

The devil bowed before Jesus, but our Lord said, "I have not come to bind you now, but to fulfill the word of My Father to give to the Church, yet to be born, the victory over all the power of the enemy." With one mighty sweep of victory our blessed Lord reached to the powers of evil, and took from the devil the keys of the kingdom. Then He arose from the grave, having opened the prison doors and set the captives free.

> *And having spoiled principalities and powers, he made a shew of them openly, triumphing over them in it* (Colossians 2:15).

Jesus said: *"Behold, I give unto you power...over all the power of the enemy"* (Luke 10:19). The devil cannot violate the authority of God which stands behind me. I am a man of authority. The powers of Satan must obey his authority. This is why I saw that the devil is a defeated foe. We only need to recognize it!

## SATAN'S GREATEST FEAR

The devil is not afraid of us, but he is afraid of Jesus. He is afraid of the badge of authority that we wear, because we do not stand alone. Behind us stands Jesus. Behind Jesus stands God the Father. With Jesus and God the Father are all the angels and a host of heavenly beings, ready to do the bidding of God Almighty!

> *And they went forth, and preached every where, the Lord working with them...* (Mark 16:20).

> *And as ye go, preach, saying, The kingdom of heaven is at hand. Heal the sick, cleanse the lepers, raise the dead, cast out devils: free ye have received, freely give* (Matthew 10:7-8).

> *Verily I say unto you, Whatsoever ye shall bind on earth shall be bound in heaven: and whatsoever ye shall loose on earth shall be loosed in heaven. Again I say unto you, That if two of you shall agree on earth as touching any thing that they shall ask, it shall be done for them of my Father which is in heaven. For where two or three are gathered together in my name, there am I in the midst of them* (Matthew 18:18-20).

Satan knows better than most Christians that they have the power and the authority to defeat him, but that does not worry him. Only when he sees them go to war against him does he become afraid.

This New Anointing revelation teaches how to use this authority and this power in a greater way. What we need to do is to act! Our enemy is located! Go to war against him in the Name of Jesus! The Church of Jesus Christ has received its marching orders to invade the kingdom of Satan.

> *And I will give unto thee the keys of the kingdom of heaven: and whatsoever thou shalt bind on earth shall be bound in heaven: and whatsoever thou shalt loose on earth shall be loosed in heaven* (Matthew 16:19).

I promise you, you are going to press forward into more prayer victories than you have ever experienced in your life as God makes this revelation real to you.

We have our enemy located. We have his complete battle plan. We know the strength of his power. We know what it will take to resist him and bring deliverance from all his works. We know that we have the power and authority of God to back us up. We have an anti-Satan defense system that he cannot penetrate if we will use it!

And we have the power and the weapons to spiritually march into Satan's territory and take it back for Christ. Now is the time to start!

## Discussion Questions

1. Have you ever given up on getting real power from God because it didn't happen immediately? Have you settled for goose bumps and emotional highs without true spiritual power?
2. If the disciples waited ten days for the baptism of the Holy Spirit, what kind of approach do you need to use in order to have your own experience of God's power?
3. Does the devil flee from you because of your ally, the One who defeated him? If not, begin claiming His victory for yourself today!

Chapter 27

# A GREAT CROWD OF WITNESSES

Paul said: "...*we also are compassed about with so great a cloud of witnesses*..." (Hebrews 12:1). The New Anointing revelation for spiritual warfare works! Thousands of witnesses have had miracle answers to prayer since they put these principles into action. This principle was the factor which led to greater, more miraculous answers to prayer in my own life and ministry.

Letters and telephone calls pour in my headquarters in San Diego every day from men and women all across the nation who have found that the New Anointing works. They have applied these truths. Their prayers have penetrated into the very spirit world, binding spirits that are evil and loosing upon their own lives and those of their loved ones the blessings that God intended for them to have.

Through the revelation of the New Anointing, God has placed in our hands the potential, the spiritual atomic bomb, to more than defeat every attack of the devil. It is not enough to have it in your grasp—you must begin to use it.

When I think of the many books written that have the power to lift people's lives to higher potentials, yet are just sitting on shelves collecting dust, it makes me realize again how I must depend upon the power of the Holy Spirit to stir people's hearts. Peter said: "...*I stir up your pure minds by way of remembrance*" (2 Peter 3:1). Do not put this book on the shelf until it has accomplished in your life what the Holy Spirit intends it to do. Let Him stir you.

## LET THE HOLY SPIRIT WORK

My dear fellow-minister, God wants to give you the joy of seeing things happen when you preach and minister. In our meetings, I have seen people give their hearts to Jesus and receive outstanding miracles of healing who were too overwhelmed by the Holy Spirit to understand a word that I said. The anointing of the Holy Spirit spoke to their hearts. They reached out from their hearts to receive God's salvation, God's healing and miracle-working power in their lives.

There have been times in our services here in North America when I have walked out onto the platform and felt the tremendous power of the Holy Spirit convicting men and women of their sins, calling them to get right with God. My first question has always been, "How many right here in this audience have never had the experience of being born again?" Hundreds of hands have been raised sincerely. They were not backsliders; they simply had never in their lives received Christ. Most of them had never been asked to receive Christ as their personal Savior.

Then in the simplest of terms, taking no more than a few minutes, I would explain the plan of salvation. Without a single emotional story, I would ask them the question, "How many would like to be born again? How many would like to receive Jesus Christ as your personal Savior?" Within moments from the time I stepped to the microphone there would be several hundred people at the altar. Many of them would stand there before me with tears streaming down their faces when five minutes before they didn't even know what it meant to be saved.

I am convinced that the Holy Spirit can do more in one split second than we can do by our efforts in a lifetime. Pastor, you don't have to walk away from your church after service with that empty, frustrated feeling, wondering seriously if you should ever go back again. Put the principles of the New Anointing into practice.

This is by no means to discount the need for preparation in prayer and in the Word. Rather, it actually intensifies your desire to be prepared. In the first service of our Dallas, Texas crusade, I came out prepared to preach a message. I had spent hours in my room in preparation and prayer. As I started to announce my subjects for the next two nights, a woman who had been in a wheelchair for ten years got up and walked down to the altar. What was I to do? Tell everybody to just hold steady and wait until after I delivered my message to receive their miracle? I really had little choice. I just had to stand back and let the Holy Spirit take over completely.

In our crusades, I actually feel the part of a spectator because I do not feel responsible for what takes place. My participation takes place back in my room in using the principles of spiritual warfare that I have described in this book. When I describe the results of the New Anointing, I am not speaking from belief or theory only, but from experience—it works! This also is the testimony of countless ministers whose lives and ministries have been completely transformed.

## Testimonies of Changed Lives

Going through customs in Vancouver, British Columbia, I met an Eskimo pastor who told me, "Brother Cerullo, I came to the Portland Crusade and Holy Spirit Teaching Seminar a year ago and my life has never been the same since."

In Tampa, Florida, a Baptist pastor reported several weeks after the crusade was over that he had not had the opportunity to preach a regular sermon in six weeks. In every service the Holy Spirit just completely took over and the Word was coming forth under the inspiration of the Spirit. Miracles and healings were literally shaking the community. The church was in a continual revival and there were immediate plans to triple the size of the sanctuary to accommodate the crowds. It literally exploded.

A pastor in Dallas, Texas, described himself as a very conservative man before the Dallas crusade. He reported afterward that he is a new preacher and he has a new church. "You just wouldn't recognize our church!" he exclaimed.

Reverend George Stormont of Manchester, England, is the perfect picture of an English gentleman with stately bearing. He pastored Beth-Shan Tabernacle in Manchester, one of the largest Pentecostal churches in the British Isles. After the New Anointing got hold of him, he needed a dry set of clothes waiting for him when he finished preaching on Sunday nights. Souls were saved in nearly every service. It wasn't the increased physical effort that produced the result, but the power of the Holy Spirit that was now so much more present in his preaching.

The New Anointing is not for ministers only. God is not a respecter of one's position in life. These principles and this authority are for all who enter into the flow of God and will claim them.

Rebecca Hagar of Denver, Colorado, was a lady who had been bound for years by the need for frequent hormone shots. (Rebecca's testimony as well as those of several others mentioned in this chapter appear in full in my book, *Miracles Happen*). If Rebecca did not have a shot every ten days, she would become so tense and overwrought that she wanted to kill somebody. She used to send her little children out to play for fear she would kill them in one of these indescribable attacks.

The fact that Rebecca was a Christian and loved God made the situation even more unbearable, as she knew this was not in harmony with the fruit of the Spirit she was supposed to exhibit in her life as a child of God. It was very frustrating. Her husband used to watch for the symptoms that told him she needed another shot. Rebecca also had a growth on her thyroid gland, was allergic to "almost everything," had varicose veins and arthritis, and had a disabled arm which had been injured during her childhood when she fell from a horse.

Rebecca came to my Holy Spirit Teaching Seminar in Denver and sat through the morning classes, drinking in God's Presence. The spiritual food lifted her to new spiritual planes. She wasn't even thinking about her physical needs, just basking in the spiritual atmosphere.

On the closing morning of the series I said, "Now we are going to put what we learned into action. I want every one of you to begin praying. I want you to come against every spirit of Satan which touches your life or those of your loved ones." As I spoke, Rebecca's hands went up and she began to exercise this power and authority from God.

She said later, "My mind was a complete blank when it came to knowing what it was I wanted to be loosed from. It never occurred to me I was under bondage to hormones, but I commanded Satan to loosen everything that affected my life." Immediately she felt the warm flow of God's Spirit in her arm and that disabled arm was loosed. The next morning while washing her face, she discovered that the growth on her thyroid was gone.

It was several days after the conference when her hormone shot was to become due, but not feeling any of the previous symptoms, Rebecca didn't take the shot. One extra day went by, then two, three, four. She waited for her husband to say something, but he didn't. A whole month went by before he asked her one morning, "Isn't it about time for your shot?"

"No, I don't take those anymore," she told him, for God had completely loosed her of the need for that medication. She no longer had an urge to kill or attacks of nerves. Through exercising of the New Anointing, she had found out that what she learned in the teaching sessions worked when put to use in her own life. The varicose veins, arthritis, and allergies were also healed.

Jean Vickers suffered from one of the worst afflictions known to medical science. Tic Douloureux is sometimes called "Devil's Pain" for good reason. Doctors say that nine out of ten people who reach the advanced stages of the painful disease attempt suicide.

The pain and suffering become so intense that everything becomes unreal. Jean, though a Christian, decided she could not cope with the pain any longer. She went into the garage to hang herself. The noose was all ready. Only a last-minute crying out to God from the very depths of her being saved her from that awful fate. Still she continued to suffer.

Several months before our crusade in Sacramento, California, the doctors began giving her a powerful new drug that took away the pain but left her in a virtual stupor. She was warned that regardless of the condition of the disease, she would be hopelessly addicted to the new drug if she ever tried to stop.

She attended the crusade services each night and she also came to the morning Holy Spirit Teaching Seminar services. Morning after morning her faith increased. Neither Jean nor I can tell you the exact moment that her miracle happened. On Thursday evening during the message on prophecy, an inner voice told her something was different and that it would not be necessary for her to take her medicine any longer. There was no mention of healing or prayer for the sick during that service, but Jean went home with an assurance that she was healed of the dreadful affliction that has baffled medical science.

Her husband warned her that if she did not take the medicine, she would be a raving maniac in the morning. Though in the natural she knew that this was true, she did not take the powerful drug that had been prescribed for her, nor did she need it. She was completely healed of the dread disease.

Mrs. Elsie Parmeland of Ridgewood, New Jersey, is typical of millions of parents across North America and around the world. Mrs. Parmeland said that her daughter was the most rebellious child you would ever meet. She hardly ever smiled. If her parents tried to touch her, she would pull away, not allowing any embrace or affection.

"When I stood in that vast auditorium," Mrs. Parmeland later related, "during the last day of your Holy Spirit Teaching Seminar in Toronto, with tears running down my cheeks, I put into action the things you have taught us. I bound the spirit of rebelliousness in my child and released the spirit of love.

"When I returned home, my daughter ran to me, threw her arms around me and said, 'Oh Mother, I missed you. I missed you.' Can you imagine what this meant to me? All I could say was, 'Praise God. Praise God.'"

When Freeda Harlow of Nocoma, Texas heard of this ministry, she began to write in her prayer requests—and God began to answer. Unable to have children of her own, Freeda talked it over with Ray and they decided to adopt one. At the orphanage they met with disappointing news—it would take about two years for them to get a child.

Freeda wrote for prayer. Six months later, the couple was in possession of the first of their new family, a five-month-old boy—but already it was a family fraught with severe problems.

When the orphanage called and told them they could pick up John, they found that he was just out of the hospital where he had been admitted at the age of three weeks with a broken arm, leg, and rib, all the result of abuse at the hands of his parents. He was bruised, undernourished, and frightened. They also discovered that he had a hernia and a ruptured navel.

When John came to the Harlows at the age of five and a half months, he was extremely frightened of people and would cling to Freeda in fear. He sometimes vomited when held by anyone else, even for a few moments.

Freeda brought John with her to my crusade in Dallas, Texas in 1974, where two things happened—Freeda received my personal teaching on the revelation of the New Anointing, and John was completely delivered of his fears. Freeda, since that time, has used the keys of the New Anointing in taking many other children into her home, some of them also victims of abuse and some considered incorrigible.

About seven million people in America are now alcoholics. There are 147 million reported cases of driving under the influence each year.[1] Linda Thomas of Tampa, Florida and Eileen Smith of Dallas, Texas both were unable to cope with the realities and pressures of life without a constant flow of liquor. Their greeting to their husbands when they came home at night was to ask them if they had brought another bottle or not.

Both of these ladies suffered physical afflictions as a result of their drinking, but still did not have the power within themselves to quit. Each of these ladies came into contact with the message of the New Anointing, and both were completely delivered from the physical and emotional need of alcohol.

Millions of dollars are spent every month in America on diets, diet pills, food, drink, doctors, clubs, clinics, and what have you to help people curb their appetites. That this revelation covers every area of our lives is evident from a letter from Linda Okerstrom of Downers Grove, Illinois, who wrote, "I want to praise the Lord for healing me of a compulsive appetite that has caused me untold heartache and suffering ever since I was eight years old. To His glory and honor I can report a weight loss of twenty-five pounds! I have never been so at peace in my life as far as dieting is concerned."

A lady in Tampa, Florida, had been divorced from her husband for five years. She still loved him and prayed every day for his salvation. He was involved in underworld activities and the conflict in the home became more than she could bear. She attended the Holy Spirit Teaching Seminar in Tampa and in the first service received enough of the New Anointing revelation to begin to use it. Her objective was her former husband. She began to bind the evil powers that held this man in their grip. Then she invited him to one of the meetings. He came and at the conclusion of my message, he came to the altar and gave his heart to Jesus.

Another family had been reunited by the power of the Holy Spirit. From Fresno, California, a lady wrote: "I attended your

Fresno Holy Spirit Teaching Seminar, and what a thrill for me! The Lord saved me from fourteen years of dope addiction and demon possession!"

Mrs. Richard Romero of Fullerton, California wrote this triumphant testimony: "For the first time in years I've been set free and delivered forever from that filthy cigarette habit. I truly experienced a beautiful victory over them. Not only did He deliver me from the cigarettes, He also removed the terrible desire." That was similar to the letter from Mr. Lynn Peterson of Watause, Tennessee, who wrote: "I just read your New Anointing article and I just quit smoking. I have been praying for the strength to quit and through your article God revealed the strength inside of me through Himself."

A Vermont woman's report is: "I recently wrote asking your advice on how to bring peace into my home. I applied your answer and wish to report that my husband's drinking and cruelty have miraculously ceased."

Mrs. Vada Gamble wrote from Gilman City, Missouri: "My husband and I have found a new area of the Spirit to live in. We have seen our building program begin (a Full Gospel Church). We have seen our only son begin to be more involved in God's service, and found the Lord's will in other things. We have both been wonderfully touched physically and spiritually."

Reverend Louise Henry, pastor of a church in Brooklyn, was so ill with a perforated ulcer and other conditions that she was too weak to pastor and the church was ready to close. Louise came to my Regional Deeper Life Conference in Lansing, Michigan. She did not receive her healing during the conference, but after she returned home, she prayed out into the Spirit and was miraculously healed. She disposed of all her medicine and went into the kitchen to prepare herself a steak dinner, although doctors had said her diet would be baby food for the rest of her life. She was also healed of an obscure disease called Webber-Christian disease which caused large egg-like nodules to grow all over her legs, and for which doctors had found no cure.

But that is not all. She plunged into her pastoral duties with new strength and the New Anointing, and within a short time her congregation had bought a new church complex which opened with 300 people present, and Louise was conducting a regular television program called, "The God Answers Prayer Program." Louise believes so strongly in the revelation of the New Anointing that she took a leave of absence from her church to enroll as one of the first students of the Morris Cerullo School of Ministry so that she would be even more effective in seeing the devil's strongholds destroyed.

## JOIN THE CLOUD!

Not just in America, but also from many countries around the world, testimonies pour in. Men and women of God who used to have "good" ministries have seen their effectiveness multiplied. We have a great cloud of witnesses. As you have read this book, you have been surrounded with this cloud of witnesses to the fact that God wants to meet your need, and that He is able to move through your life and ministry to bring Christ's deliverance to others.

Nothing in life happens by chance. This book in your hands will revolutionize your life if you will let it. It is now up to you—it is in your hands. I have delivered the revelation that God has given to me under the anointing of the Holy Spirit. I believe that you can feel that anointing as you read this book.

I pray that you not only will be a hearer of the Word, but a doer also—that the message you have received will cause you immediately to see the results of this message in your life. I pray that everyone who reads this book will become more than a conqueror for Christ. God gives you New Anointing in your life, and will now bring you into prayer victories you have never before experienced.

God bless you! *Amen!*

## Discussion Questions

1. As you read through the testimonies of God's power changing lives, which ones stand out the most to you and why?
2. Imagine the power of the New Anointing in your own life—envision your own testimony added to this list. Now go after it!

### Note

1. "Injury Prevention and Control: Motor Vehicle Safety," Centers for Disease Control and Prevention, October 18, 2011, How Big Is the Problem?, accessed July 13, 2012, http://www.cdc.gov/Motorvehiclesafety/Impaired_Driving/impaired-drv_factsheet.html.

Epilogue

# GOD'S GOT AN ARMY

The only real ending for a book on spiritual strategy for defeating the devil is found in the final chapters of the greatest Book, the Holy Bible, where it is written of the loser:

> *And the devil that deceived them was cast into the lake of fire and brimstone, where the beast and the false prophet are, and shall be tormented day and night for ever and ever* (Revelation 20:10).

And where it is written of the victors: *"He that overcometh shall inherit all things; and I will be his God, and he shall be my son"* (Revelation 21:7). We have read "the back of the book," and we know what the ending is. Satan will be completely defeated and sent into everlasting torment, while God's victorious people will enter into everlasting joy with our Lord.

I believe that time is very near at hand. Yet, until it is actually accomplished, the battle goes on—the battle in which an army of men and women, raised up by God, are tearing out of the hands of the enemy the souls of millions of people around the world, people who need the help of our prayers and labor of love that they might enter with us into these joys.

God has such an army—an army that is on the march. How grateful I am that so much of the Army is composed of dedicated men and women from many nations of the world who have found added strength and motivation for the battle of faith through the Morris Cerullo Schools of Ministry.

The truths in this book are truths which I have long taught and practiced in more than 56 years of ministry around the world. During this time, I personally have taught these keys of spiritual warfare, and now more than 1.3 million ministers and other Christian leaders, many of them in Third World nations, are continuing the teaching.

## PLEASE TEACH ME

It was in the city of Porto Alegre, Brazil in 1962, where I was holding a crusade service at the Exposition Grounds that God impressed upon me the urgency and the importance of unifying His people into an Army to take the nations of the world for Him. About 50,000 people were present for the crusade service on this particular day as I began to minister. I had been at the microphone for only a short time when suddenly a tremendous pain shot through my chest. I had never had heart trouble before, but I thought I was having a heart attack.

The pulpit for this meeting was just a board nailed on the railing of the platform—very rough and not very substantial—but I grabbed for it and held on to keep from falling. My whole body was doubled up with pain and my thoughts were racing. "Am I going to die? Is God going to take me home now?" I finally was able to reach out my hand to my overseas crusade director and pull him over to the microphone. Not able to explain the whole situation to him in a split second, I said to him, "Please, you close the meeting. It is impossible for me to go on. Something has happened. I must get back to my hotel."

The automobile in which I rode in from the hotel to the Exposition Grounds for the services was parked behind the platform and I literally fell into it. The driver took me back to my hotel room and I did not even take time to remove my wet clothes. I just fell on my face before God on the floor of my hotel room. "Lord," I asked, "are You taking me home?"

Even lying there on the floor in great pain, I realized that God did not need the help of a heart attack to take me home. He could just take my spirit out of my body. I did not need, nor want, to suffer some disease or affliction.

God soon let me know that this pain was not for the purpose of my homegoing. As I lay there, the pain lifted completely and it has never occurred again. I have never had any heart trouble. As I realized the pain was gone, God came into my room and He spoke to me very clearly and very directly. He said, *"Son, I have permitted this to happen to you for a purpose."*

I said, "Lord, please teach me." I was only thirty years old at the time, but already God had given me one of the most successful ministries in the history of the world. Yet, I knew there is always more to be learned.

In answer to my plea for God to teach me what He wanted me to know through this particular experience, God asked me a very peculiar question. He said, "Morris, what do you want out of this life?"

I thought to myself, "Now, that is very strange for God to ask me."

God knows our thoughts. He also knows the intents of our hearts. In all of these years of evangelism on the foreign fields and throughout the world without a break, I have never disobeyed God. Every time God told me to go somewhere, I went. Every time He told me to do something, I did it. I never disobeyed Him. The lives of myself, my wife, Theresa, and our family have always been totally on the altar. That is why I found God's question so very strange.

"God, why would You ask me that?" I asked Him. "Knowing the dedication and knowing the consecration that I have made to You, why would You ask me what I want out of this life?"

From traveling the length and breadth of this world, I had seen the many needs of this world. I knew that if I preached three times a day every day of my life I could never reach the world for Christ.

There are six billion people living on the face of the earth. One man, or even several select evangelists, can never get to all of these nations.

## WHAT'S THE ANSWER?

Many people have supposed that television is the answer to worldwide evangelism, but they do not consider that 80 percent of the world's population live in rural areas, and many of them are too remote to receive any television exposure. Even though there are great cities such as Manila in the Philippines and Nairobi and Lagos in Africa, three or four miles outside of these places, there is abject poverty. Most places do not have electricity or running water, much less television. They have none of the conveniences that belong to the population located in the United States, Canada, and Great Britain.

Also, there is no way to reach all of Europe by television because in many European nations television is owned and totally controlled by the government. Television is a great medium to reach the United States and Canada, but we can never evangelize the world through those means. That wasn't the answer.

In 1962, when this encounter with God occurred, I already knew what the answer was, because I had traveled from country to country and I had seen the tremendous needs of the people. I knew what God was probing for with His question.

There are many people who want to leave behind some kind of monument to themselves, some tribute to their particular abilities—a building, a school, a monument—something tangible. But there was one thing I wanted out of life and God knew it. I said, "Lord, there is only one thing that I ask of You in this world—only one thing. Give me the ability—give me the anointing—to take what You have given to me and to be able to communicate it to someone else."

That was the earnest cry of my heart, because the only way we will ever reach this world for God is if God raises up trained and motivated men and women, full of the power of Holy Spirit, who will go into the villages and countryside of their own countries and evangelize their own nations. I saw clearly that the trained and motivated Nation is the key to reaching the nations of this world for God.

So this was my request to God: "Give me the ability to take what You have given me, the power and anointing that is upon my ministry, and give me the ability to communicate that to others." That is what I wanted out of life.

God said to me as I lay there on the floor in 1962: *"Son, build Me an Army."*

What a charge and what a challenge! But God has helped me to build such an Army. He has given me an anointing of apostolic leadership which has been translated into an Army of recruits to do His great work around the world. For years now, we have been building God an Army in Africa, in Asia, in India, in South America, in the Philippines—everywhere I have been privileged to go and minister for our Lord, Jesus Christ.

I have been invited to nation after nation, and every time I consented to go to a certain country, I always insisted that one of the conditions was that I could meet with the national ministers and share with them on as personal a level as possible the keys to effective evangelism which God has put into my hands.

This outreach grew and developed tremendously over the years. Still it was not enough. The invitations to come to the nations of the world continued to flow in until I could not have met all the invitations that lay on my desk even in ten years, or many lifetimes.

Then, instead of diminishing the demand, God increased the vision. That is when the School of Ministry was born. God put it into my mind and into my heart to build a School of Ministry right in my hometown area of San Diego, where people from all nations could come from all over the world and learn these truths in a central place. They in turn would disperse to all corners of the world bearing these same truths to share with others.

With the vision, God also gave me a great sense of urgency. When engineers, architects, and contractors all explained to me that it would take at least three years to build a school, the urgency in my heart would not let me accept that answer. I began a search for an empty school or campus with nearby housing where the School of Ministry could begin immediately at an interim location while we built something suitable.

God knew the urgency of the hour even more than I did, and He had the answer. Suddenly—dramatically and miraculously—God opened the way to acquire a fully equipped and operating hotel facility with 500 rooms and generous classroom facilities. The story of how the financial obligations were met to permit the acquisition of this facility also is staggering—but again God met the need.

Even as I wondered how to present the need and challenge to our friends and partners so that the magnitude of the vision would not overwhelm them, God spoke new assurance to my heart. I was travailing in prayer alone in my hotel room just before going into a service in Washington, D.C., when God spoke these words to me which have been a source of great and continuing encouragement:

He said to me: *"Don't look to the bigness of your need, look to the bigness of your God. Your circumstances are hindered to seeing My abilities. If you keep your eyes on your circumstances, the devil will use your circumstances to defeat you and accuse the Word of God—the written and the Living Word. Your victory is in keeping your eyes on the bigness of your God and His ability. He has promised to take you step by step by step—not all at once but step by step and—each step will be a miracle!"*

## Miracle After Miracle

Step by step God has led; each step has been a miracle. That is why, within a matter of a very few months, the down payment for the facility changed hands and I was presented with the keys to the facility and a deed of trust on October 2, 1978.

And another great miracle coupled with the dedication and ability of those whom God had raised up to help—the Morris Cerullo

School of Ministry opened its doors to more than 500 students only three months later on January 1, 1979!

Still another miracle! We were able to intensify the keys of effective evangelism in the apostolic power of the Holy Spirit into six high-speed learning months, stressing not only knowledge, but the motivation and power of the Holy Spirit.

Then, another miracle. God allowed us to further intensify the next session of the School of Ministry—and the next—into three-month sessions. Men and women came from more than 40 nations of the world for each session with the promise and the pledge that they would take into their hands and hearts the keys for reaching their nations, and that they would return and pass these same keys to at least 100 other people! God's law of multiplication for building an Army!

Each life that passes into the school and is revolutionized for Jesus Christ and goes out again to take the world for Him is a new miracle. It is no wonder that the theme songs selected for the Schools of Ministry were: "God's Got an Army" and "It Is the Time to Take the Kingdom!"

Beloved, you, too, no matter who you are, are a vital part of God's Army. We must all be disciples. The hour is now—the kingdom is the Lord's: *"Whose voice then shook the earth: but now he hath promised, saying, Yet once more I shake not the earth only, but also heaven"* (Hebrews 12:26).

Still I have not been satisfied. There is still an urgency. We must enlist others by the tens of thousands to learn these keys, to absorb them, to use them, and most of all to teach them to others.

# COME MARCH WITH US IN GOD'S VICTORIOUS ARMY!

Not one of us can grow spiritually, multiply our faithfulness in the Lord, and launch sustained, victorious warfare on Satan's strongholds if we are alone. We need each other! He has shown me a way to do this through God's Victorious Army, a monthly ministry that is literally building an Army for God throughout the world. *God is calling you to join us!*

## GOD HAS HEARD YOUR CRIES

God has heard your cry for greater knowledge of Him, and your cry to be a vital part of His end-time plan.

To answer these cries, He has given me a way to teach you (right in your own home) how to manifest the same proof-producing power that anoints our nationals to take their countries for Christ! *As a member of God's Victorious Army, each month you will receive:*

- A power-packed lesson in spiritual warfare and personal growth, written with specific steps for spiritual growth.
- Instructions on intercessory prayer, to break down enemy strongholds throughout the world.

- Special sections to help you see how God is preparing His Bride to fulfill prophetic destiny.
- Periodically, you will receive special gifts of tapes and other ministry tools.

## YOUR MONTHLY GIFT PLANTS EXPLOSIVE SEEDS!

Beloved, you can't go to Africa, South America or Central America, Mexico, Brazil, Asia, or India. But through your monthly gift you are reaching these nations to raise up an Army for God. The men and women you sponsor are your hands and feet in areas of the world that are now closed to missionaries.

## TESTIMONIES

**Richard Omenako, Accra, Ghana**

Son of an earthly king, now son of the King of kings:

> My earthly father was a king who ruled over 600,000 people in Ghana. Now my heavenly Father is my King of kings! I give honor to the Lord Jesus Christ that I am part of God's Victorious Army.
>
> Before I went to Morris Cerullo School of Ministry, I had only one church of about 80 people. But when Dr. Cerullo came to Ghana, my life changed. Now I have five churches of 2,700 members. I have also set up an organization to unify 1,750 churches. Now God's Victorious Army in Africa consists of born-again Presbyterians, Methodists, Pentecostals and Baptists…all marching in unity and taking the land for Jesus Christ!

**Benjamin Munthe, Medan, Indonesia**

Ten brought in ten thousand in one year!

How I thank God for God's Victorious Army which is now marching across Indonesia.

I have put into practice the proof-producing principles of the School of Ministry. Using these strategies, I started an "I-Care" prayer center in my home.

At first, there were just ten people involved. But in one year the number increased to 100. Then I conducted my first crusade in Medan, where 10,000 people filled the sports hall! Thousands were saved as God performed many miracles and wonders.

**Alejandro Morales, Mexico City, Mexico**

From traditionalism to evangelism!

Even though I attended a traditional Bible school for three years, and had a heart to serve God, I was still confused, angry and even rebellious.

Then the Lord miraculously opened the doors for me to attend the Morris Cerullo School of Ministry. In this school, Brother Cerullo taught me how to use the weapons of our warfare...to be a good soldier for Jesus Christ and pull down the strongholds of Satan. I graduated a *new man.*

My first act of faith when I arrived back in Mexico was to claim the jungles of Oaxaca for Jesus. By using the plan of spiritual warfare that I learned in the School of Ministry, a fearless army of Proof Producers was raised up in *every village I passed through.*

Now the Oaxaca jungles have 13 churches, some with as many as 300 members! Praise God that God's Victorious Army is *you.* It is me!

**Dean Lane, Phoenix, Arizona**

Alcoholics for Christ—Dean Lane testifies:

Since becoming a member of God's Victorious Army, God has opened the doors for me to start an "Alcoholics for Christ" ministry. (They) are responding mightily to the Word of God.

I am teaching from the Victory Miracle Library to as many people as I possibly can. The whole church is becoming involved in supporting this ministry. We go down to the park every Saturday, and so many are grateful for this opportunity to learn about God's Word. We are getting to minister to many, many people and see them gain deliverance from alcoholism.

The wonderful thing is that we are able to share not just a new direction with people, but a whole new way of life, as they begin walking with Jesus!

*The same anointing that God has given our nationals can come upon you, week by week, month by month, in God's Victorious Army!*

# ABOUT DR. MORRIS CERULLO

Dr. Cerullo has also authored more than 160 books. Few ministers have had such an impact on the destiny of the nations of the world. Morris Cerullo's life has been sacrificially dedicated to training and spiritually equipping pastors, lay people, and evangelists to reach their nations for Christ with a supernatural endowment of God's Power.

**Morris Cerullo World Evangelism**

P.O. Box 85277
San Diego, CA 92186

Phone: (858) 277-2200

E-mail: morriscerullo@mcwe.com

Website: www.mcwe.com

For 24 hours a day, 7 days a week prayer, call: (858) HELPLINE

**Morris Cerullo World Evangelism of Canada**

P.O. Box 3600
Concord, Ontario L4K-1B6

Phone: (905) 669-1788

**Morris Cerullo World Evangelism of Great Britain**

P.O. Box 277
Hemel Hempstead, HERTS HP2-7DH 44

Phone: (0)1 442 232432

# OTHER BOOKS BY DR. MORRIS CERULLO

*The Prophet's Mantle*

*Christ, Your Healer*

*How to Break Satan's Cycle of Defeat*